Andy Kempe

D1440075

St

Dra

First edition published in 1997 by:
Stanley Thornes (Publishers) Ltd

Second edition published in 2002 by:
Nelson Thornes Ltd
Delta Place
27 Bath Road
CHELTENHAM
GL53 7TH
United Kingdom

02 03 04 05 06 / 10 9 8 7 6 5 4 3 2 1

A catalogue record for this book is available from the British Library

ISBN 0-7487-6509-7

Illustrations by Mick Stubbs and Mark Walker
Page make-up by Alden Press
Printed and bound in Croatia by Zrinski

Contents

CONTENTS

Section four   Dramatic characters

Section five   Experiencing the production

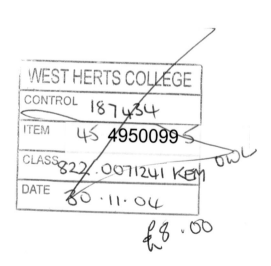

Teacher's introduction

Plays are different from novels. That seems an obvious statement to make but for teachers of English and Drama it has a number of implications for classroom practice that this book will address.

The 'traditional' way of teaching plays has been very close to the ways in which novels have been taught. The focus has been on the narrative and the characters. The students' comprehension of the play has tended to be tested by asking what happens in the play and what the characters' attitudes towards the central drama and each other appear to be. Creative extension tasks purporting to help students gain an insight into the play have often been centred on building up profiles of the characters as if they were real people. Writing extracts from the character's personal diary, writing letters they may have sent, improvising or writing new scenes around the drama, reporting on the play as if an outside agency such as a newspaper and so on: all have been the stock in trade of many follow-up sections of school editions and imaginative English and Drama teachers themselves. Exercises such as these have many values in engaging the students with the story and issues of the play, but they may be limited in helping students actually understand the way the play works as a medium which is, essentially, quite different from the novel.

Most secondary age students already have considerable knowledge of the ways in which novels work. As young children they are read stories and move on through reading examples of a vast and excellent body of children's literature available to the point where they can tackle 'adult' novels. Even if the structures of such books have not been directly addressed by their teachers, familiarity with the novel form will have taught them to expect certain things to happen in certain ways. Children's progression in understanding drama as an art form has often been more haphazard than this. Their first encounter with drama is likely to be through their own largely unstructured imaginative play. It's quite a jump from this to presenting themselves publicly in the annual primary school play where for the first time they may have specific lines to learn and performance skills to adopt. In many cases, children's next encounter with drama in its scripted form has been in the secondary school when they have been required to start analysing scripts in terms of their literary content. While young people can be said to have experienced making, performing and responding to drama through such a personal career, the degree to which they have been able to make productive links between these areas of activity is clearly limited by the disparate nature of the way each has been encountered. As a result, secondary age students have often found it difficult to see how improvisations and role plays undertaken in a drama lesson relate to the study of plays in English or the preparations undertaken for public presentations.

However, the National Curriculum for English now includes the requirement for children at Key Stages 1 and 2 to read playscripts. The National Literacy Strategy similarly supports the structured introduction of dramatic literature to children in primary schools. Children are thus increasingly entering secondary school with a working knowledge of how plays are different from novels both in the way they are presented on the page and how they may be brought to life in performance. Nevertheless, it is still often the case that students starting KS3 will have an understanding of how playscripts work that is, inevitably perhaps, somewhat rudimentary. This means that secondary school teachers of English and Drama can have quite a task in meeting the requirements of the National Curriculum for English at Key Stages 3 and 4 in this area.

For many students at Key Stage 3, the prospect of studying a whole play as a formal classroom activity will still represent a new venture. Scripts are often tackled by reading aloud in class, sometimes acting out scenes, and moving on to the kinds of comprehension and creative extension tasks mentioned above. At KS3 and 4 students are required to study two plays by Shakespeare and other drama by major playwrights. There is now an increased emphasis on studying plays in ways that will extend students' understanding of drama in performance. This implies the need to consider how plays are directed, the role of design in production and how actors go about interpreting and portraying characters. The requirements for Speaking and Listening in GCSE English similarly indicate a need for teachers to attend to different ways of using the voice and drawing attention to the way in which audiences decode what they hear. The insistence of GCSE Drama specifications that students study substantial playscripts further supports the need for teachers of Drama and English to adopt a highly focused and well-structured approach to teaching the way plays are created, performed and received.

The questions underlying the practical approaches offered in this book are:
1 Is it appropriate to start a study of dramatic literature by studying complete texts as sophisticated and challenging as those of Shakespeare and the kinds of major playwrights represented in the English National Curriculum (Marlowe, Priestley, Shaw and Sheridan)?
2 What support do English teachers need in order to become familiar enough with the different elements of performance to guide their students towards an understanding of plays as a basis from which to create a performance rather than completed works of literature?
3 What support do Drama teachers need in order to become familiar enough with the literary devices employed by dramatists to guide their students towards an understanding of the art of the playwright?

Plays are what might be termed 'procedural texts'. That is, unlike a novel which is read in order to discover what happens next, plays are read in order to discover how things happen. They are, with some exceptions, a sort of blueprint which must be interpreted in order to realise them as performance texts. An actor will read a play with an eye on how she might perform a character and make any apparent development of that character believable and coherent in the performance. A director will read a play with an eye to what the underlying concept is to her and how she will use all the elements of theatrical presentation to realise this. A designer will be picking out the technical challenges of the play and asking how she might tackle these in an aesthetic way which enhances rather than impedes the integrity of the script as visualised by the director. Rather like a group of engineers, architects, financial managers and potential customers poring over the blueprints for a new building, those involved in the theatre will look at a playscript and ask 'how will this thing be constructed and presented? How much will it cost? What will it look like? Why do we need it? How will people receive it?' Unlike a blueprint for a piece of engineering, though, a playscript will not provide all of the answers. If scripts really were like blueprints then every performance of the play would be exactly the same. The fact that quite the opposite is the case indicates that certain key elements are missing from the plan. These elements include those who read, perform and watch the play, each and every one of whom will add something of themselves to the process of production and reception.

This is not to say that playscripts do not have an aesthetic quality in their own right. The playwright's language in particular may be pleasing in its use of the sound qualities of words and the imagery they suggest. The story may well be as engaging as many a novel. But every time the play is produced, the different interpretations of the actors, director and designers will effectively change the parameters of how an audience will interpret the play for themselves. To understand a play in terms of its potential in performance therefore demands that its readers are aware of their own position in relation to the text. This requires learning not only how to read for story and character development, but learning how to visualise the different ways in which the finished production may affect subsequent interpretations.

Finally, a further word about children's experience of drama in performance. It might actually be true to say that young people today encounter more drama in performance in one week than most of their counterparts a century ago would have seen in a lifetime. Through television, film and to a lesser extent radio, young people are in fact very familiar with many of the conventions of performance. In order to acquaint students with the dynamics of drama written for the stage, it is extremely useful to draw on this vernacular knowledge of performance. Indeed, by doing so the teacher would be covering those other aspects of the English National Curriculum which require students to be introduced to a wide range of media and how texts are changed when adapted to different media.

The units in this book are designed not only to teach young people new skills for reading and enjoying plays, but to make explicit to them the skills they already possess and offer them ways of utilising these in the context of their studies in English and Drama. The discrete yet linked activities suggested in this book will build up students' appreciation of drama in performance and enable them to refer to specific activities in their written accounts. Such a level of detail will be helpful in achieving the higher grades when writing reviews of plays, commenting on their own performances and assessing the effectiveness of different practical approaches; an invaluable grounding for those students who wish to go on to study Drama and Theatre Studies at 'A' Level.

About this book

The extracts and exercises in this book have been selected to help secondary school students read plays in a way that will enhance their understanding of drama in performance and so recognise how dramatic literature is different from other literary forms. The ideas are presented in the knowledge that it is rarely possible to take students to the theatre or to perform whole plays for themselves. Even if these options were viable they would still be problematic, as seeing one production of a play is unlikely to expose the way the meanings of playscripts are mediated in performance unless further close study of the script is made through using comparative performance texts. Similarly, simply showing television or film versions of plays is unlikely to give an insight into how the play works on stage; in fact, it may even encourage a false impression of the play because of the accepted norm of using naturalistic forms in these media. Even just taking the class off to a well-equipped drama studio to test out how different elements of theatre presentation might affect interpretation of the play is often logistically difficult.

The approach offered here is to engage students in a practical approach to extracts taken from a wide range of plays. By using accessible examples in the first instance, the students are directed towards seeing how major playwrights from different eras, including Shakespeare, have also used the same elements of playwriting.

This book is divided into five sections, each dealing with a different aspect of reading and writing dramatic literature. Each section of the book contains:
● an introduction which explains and focuses the aims and contents of the units in that section and gives an indication of the extracts used;
● a number of ideas for discussion, writing, improvisation and rehearsal tasks which may be used individually or in sequence;

● key words, printed in bold, which are gathered and explained for quick refer-ence in a glossary at the end of the book.

There is no requirement to work through each section in any particular order. Each section could be used as a coherent unit of work in its own right. Teachers may want to use just some of the extracts and ideas offered in each section to support work being undertaken on another whole script, or use them to differ-entiate classroom activities according to the different abilities of the students.

In most cases the suggested tasks could be tackled by the students with mini-mal assistance from the class teacher. However, drama is a social art form. It is about people and the best understanding of how drama works will involve peo-ple working together. What follows is a quick reference guide to the sort of activ-ities we have used in the study of plays. Some, as you will see, require more teacher involvement than others.

Basic questions

The types of questions one can ask about a play are actually quite limited:
● Who wrote the play and when?
● What characters are in the play?
● What is the storyline?
● Where is it set?
● What seem to be the major issues in the play?
● How is tension built up in the play?
● How does the context in which the play was written and the context in which we are receiving it affect our understanding?

In the case of some plays we could discuss how the play should be performed but in most cases it is better to ask how it might be performed. So, we might ask:
● To what extent does the play reveal something about the context in which it was written?
● What practical constraints are implicit in the play's form?
● In what way is it relevant or interesting for us?
● How do we understand the actions that a character is making or the rela-tionship that character has with others?
● Does the play appear to have any metaphoric or symbolic value? Could it work at more than one level in performance?

The work you might do on a play would largely depend on whether or not the class had seen or read it. You may just want to use the narrative as a stimulus for the students' own creative work. On the other hand, you may be looking for practical, accessible activities that will increase the students' insight into how the written text could be translated into a performance.

TEACHER'S INTRODUCTION

First responses

An alternative to asking the kind of comprehension type questions which suggest that there is only one meaning of the text, is to find tasks that allow students to state what they have seen in it personally. Activities that will draw on their personal response will include:
- re-telling the story in pairs or groups
- pinpointing moments that surprised and delighted them
- jotting down questions that were raised but not answered by the text
- engaging with a cloze exercise in which the story is re-told with key words missing
- re-telling parts of the story from a different perspective (how would a servant from Elsinore explain to a friend what had been going on at the castle?)
- drawing maps or diagrams of the play's location
- making a storyboard of selected scenes
- making a frozen image to show what the play meant to them as a whole, or creating a number of still images to show how the atmosphere of the play changed as it went on
- using movement to suggest the tone and rhythm of the play
- pausing at key moments to improvise predictions of what could happen next.

Written tasks

There are a great many extension tasks which can be employed to help students show what they already know and understand about a text, be it a play, poem or novel. These are useful for many reasons in that they demand that the students engage their own creativity. We would reiterate, though, that many of these, while valid as exercises in written English, can be limited in giving the students a real insight into how plays work in performance. Nevertheless, you might try:
- writing newspaper headlines and stories ('New Sighting of Ghost at Elsinore!')
- letters from or to characters
- epitaphs and obituaries
- prayers spoken by a character at key moments in the play
- school reports for key characters
- diary or filofax entries for characters
- writing additional or 'missing' scenes.

There are, however, some written tasks that can really help students show their understanding of the play as a performance text. For example:
- writing notes about a character which would be useful for the casting director
- writing reviews of actual or imagined performances ('Space Age "Hamlet" Fails to Lift Off!')

• writing notes from an actor's or director's point of view on preparing for a performance

• producing programme notes on the play from a historical or contemporary viewpoint.

Character work

There is a delicate balance to be sought in working on a play's characters. Suggesting that the characters have their own psychological reality can lead to the fatuous 'How many children had Lady Macbeth?' kind of question. A play's characters are open to interpretation, as any comparative study of performance will show. More usefully, students might consider the functions the characters appear to serve in the play; how they relate to each other and how we, the audience, are being encouraged to relate to them. You might try the following exercises:

• **Role on the wall**: this involves drawing a simple outline of the character which is filled with notes on what we actually know about the character from the text. Around the outline students are asked to write what they assume about the character and/or what their personal response to the character is.

• **Hot seating**: students ask one of the characters (played by either the teacher or another student) questions about their attitudes. This technique is especially productive if the questions are asked from another character's point of view, e.g. 'Hamlet, I don't want to go and live in a nunnery! Why did you tell me to?'

• **The character pot**: the students sit in a circle. One student crosses the circle and addresses another as if she were a chosen character. That student then sets off across the circle and says a line to a third student and so on. So, for example, imagine Hamlet is the focus of the study: the first student might cross to another and say, 'Basically, I think you're just a selfish brat.' The second student sets off and says, 'It must have been very difficult for you, losing your father like that.' This activity can be made more sophisticated by giving the character the right to reply or insisting that the statement is made from another character's point of view, as in the hot-seating task.

• **Imaging relationships**: groups are asked to show physically the tensions and/or the relationships between characters. A related task would be to use the space to show how the students relate to a character as themselves or as other characters. For example, a chair is placed in the middle of the room to represent Hamlet. The students are asked to adopt a position in relation to the chair – Hamlet's father might stand facing his son, Claudius might crouch behind the chair, hand ready to throttle him, Ophelia might stand at a distance to one side looking over her shoulder at him. The way students tackle this is fascinating and can lead to very fruitful discussions about how they understand the relationships and how stage space can be used to convey this.

● **Finding yourself**: students are given different lines from the play. Their task is to mill around the room saying their line and listening carefully to the lines being said back. Can they identify which other students have lines spoken by the same character but at a different moment in the play?

● **Conscience alley**: a moment is chosen when a character makes an important decision. The students form two lines and the teacher or another student walks down between the two lines listening to the different voices that the character might hear in her head before making her decision.

● **Re-setting the lines in a new context**: students are given an extract to study for genre and style. They are asked to select no more than four consecutive lines from the extract and to 'hide' them in a new scene of their own devising. The task inevitably demands that they assimilate the style and language of the original.

● **Packing up**: the students are asked to imagine that a character is moving house. A box or case is placed in the middle of the circle and students, in role as the chosen character, pretend to pack the box one by one. What would the character take with her?

● **The family album**: if a character had kept a series of photographs of key moments in their life, what would those photographs show? The students make still images of those moments, which may come from the play or beyond it.

Plot and structure

Plot and structure cannot be adequately studied through extracts. If you are studying a whole play, however, then it is essential that attention is paid to the way the whole thing hangs together and progresses. We have found that the following ideas work very well:

● **The quick read**: rather than plodding through the complete play with the whole class over a number of weeks, try splitting the class into small groups and giving each a different section of the play to read. Their task is to note, on slips of paper, the main events of that section, though at this point they will not know how those events relate to the overall narrative. This leads onto …

● **Mapping**: the class gather together and each group re-tells what happened in their section of the play in order. The slips of paper are laid out on a long sheet of paper. Lines are drawn between events that seem to relate to each other. In this way the class can very quickly achieve an overview of the narrative line and the main characters. An example of the first part of a 'map' of Lin Coghlan's play *A Feeling in My Bones* is shown opposite.

● **Scenes we'd like to see**: students write a brief description of a scene that might be inserted into the play. The description is passed to another group who improvises it.

● **What's going on elsewhere**: this is similar to the exercise above but takes Tom Stoppard's approach from *Rosencrantz and Guildenstern Are Dead* in which

Map of A *Feeling in My Bones*

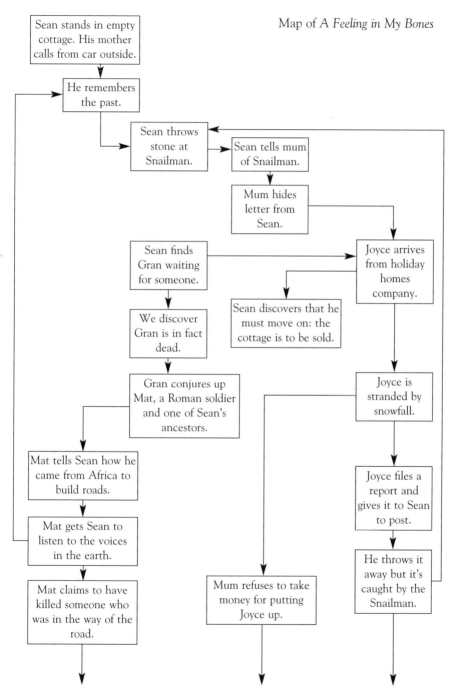

Sean stands in empty cottage. His mother calls from car outside.

He remembers the past.

Sean throws stone at Snailman.

Sean tells mum of Snailman.

Mum hides letter from Sean.

Sean finds Gran waiting for someone.

We discover Gran is in fact dead.

Sean discovers that he must move on: the cottage is to be sold.

Joyce arrives from holiday homes company.

Gran conjures up Mat, a Roman soldier and one of Sean's ancestors.

Joyce is stranded by snowfall.

Mat tells Sean how he came from Africa to build roads.

Mat gets Sean to listen to the voices in the earth.

Joyce files a report and gives it to Sean to post.

Mat claims to have killed someone who was in the way of the road.

Mum refuses to take money for putting Joyce up.

He throws it away but it's caught by the Snailman.

characters on the edge of the action tell their story or main characters are seen in new situations ('Every exit is an entrance somewhere else').

● **Reconstructing passages:** students are given a short section of text which has been cut up into individual lines. The task is to reassemble the scene. The sophistication of this task obviously depends upon the complexity of the scene chosen. With younger groups the focus will most likely be on narrative sequence, whereas older groups could focus on the language style of different characters or the action implied in the lines. An example of a suitable piece for this exercise is 'The Betrayal' from Brecht's *Fears and Miseries of the Third Reich*. The text is given below.

A man and a woman are standing by the door listening. They are very pale.

WOMAN   They've got to the ground floor.

MAN   Not quite.

WOMAN   They've smashed the banisters. He'd already passed out when they dragged him out of his flat.

MAN   I simply said the sound of foreign broadcasts didn't come from   5
here.

WOMAN   That wasn't all you said.

MAN   I said nothing more than that.

WOMAN   Don't look at me that way. If you said nothing more, then
you said nothing more.   10

MAN   That's not the point.

WOMAN   Why not go round to the police and make a statement saying nobody called there on Saturday?

Pause

MAN   Catch me going to the police. It was inhuman, the way they
were treating him.   15

WOMAN   He asked for it. What's he want to meddle in politics for?

MAN   They didn't have to rip his jacket though. Our sort isn't that well off for clothes.

WOMAN   What's a jacket more or less?

MAN   They didn't have to rip it.   20

from *Fears and Miseries of the Third Reich*

● **Hot spots:** focus on just one scene or short extract. Ask the students to pick out a line or action that seems to mark the most tense moment. Discussing how dramatic tension is achieved is a very important element of working on plays. Tension has many forms and can only be really understood in the context of the whole play.

● **Time and tension lines**: students make a graph to show how the tension of the play changes for different characters, and indeed the audience, as it progresses.

● **The Readers' Digest production**: using the notes created from the mapping exercise, students present a highly edited version of the play through still images, short improvisations and use of selected lines.

● **The flat book**: the whole play text is mounted onto card and displayed on the classroom wall. Map pins are used to identify key lines in the text. Different colours may be used for different themes and joined by coloured wool. For example, the text of Measure for Measure could show how the themes of sexual hypocrisy, political corruption and honour are apparent in what different characters say. This device is an extremely useful tool for revision and formal essay writing. You will also be surprised how displaying a play like this changes students' perceptions of it (the average Shakespeare play can be pasted onto just four sheets of sugar paper).

Design and production

Our assumption is that for most teachers it is extremely difficult to make a study of a play that culminates in an actual production. Nevertheless, there are a number of tasks that can be set in the classroom which address aspects of production. For example:

● designing the costumes of different characters
● designing settings, posters and programmes
● finding appropriate music for a soundtrack
● casting the play by thinking of well-known actors who might suit the characters
● ascribing different colours to scenes according to where they are set and what atmosphere they convey
● taking this further and writing lighting plots for certain scenes
● producing extracts of the play on cassette or video recorder to explore how the different media are constrained
● storyboarding short extracts for filming
● photographing actors or set models to show lighting effects.

And finally ...

Don't forget that students might just enjoy watching or reading plays for themselves, talking about them, rehearsing scenes from them or improvising around the story and themes.

Section one   How are plays different from novels?

Section summary

1 Introduction

Extracts from *Cat's Eye* by Margaret Atwood and *The Catcher in the Rye* by J.D. Salinger reveal the way writers of novels introduce characters and adopt a particular 'voice' to tell their story. An extract from John Steinbeck's novel *Of Mice and Men* is then compared to his play version of the same story to high-light some of the fundamental differences between plays and novels as texts.

2 Reading for story

Two short extracts from Ben Payne's *The Last Laugh* and Shakespeare's *Romeo and Juliet* are set against previews from the *Radio Times* to illustrate how know-ing the basic storyline can be helpful in preparing an audience for the play to come.

3 The plot

A practical exercise using *Romeo and Juliet* is suggested to help students see how a plot is created through using a number of 'stepping stones'.

4 Setting the scene

Extracts from Philip Pullman's *Sherlock Holmes and the Limehouse Horror*, Keith Dewhurst's *Lark Rise to Candleford* and Tennessee Williams' *The Glass Menagerie* draw attention to the different ways in which playwrights help an audience settle into the world of dramatic fiction.

5 Special strategies

This unit introduces a number of special terms, then focuses on the technique of using a narrator, with an example from Brian Woolland's play *Gulliver*.

6 *Chorus*

This unit follows on closely to the preceding one and uses extracts from *Oedipus the King* by Sophocles, *Murder in the Cathedral* by T.S. Eliot, *Blood Wedding* by Lorca and *My Mother Said I Never Should* by Charlotte Keatley to illustrate how the story of the play may be both told and commented on in choric ways.

7 *Dramatic irony*

In the final unit of this section, the different aspects of plot, character and setting are pulled together through an exploration of a scene from *The Rivals* by R.B. Sheridan. The importance of remembering that an audience is present while the play is in progress is stressed.

Unit 1   Introduction

What is a script?

The first thing we want to say about playscripts is that they are always about something. Many of them – but not all – tell a story. You don't need us to tell you that different stories appeal to different people – just try it for yourself.

● Jot down three dramas that you have seen recently that you really enjoyed. They may have been performed on stage, television or film. Give one reason why you liked each one.

● Compare your notes with at least three other people's. How do you feel about their choices? How do you feel about their reaction to what you have selected?

The word 'script' simply means that something has been written down. Not all dramas have a script. If you are lucky enough to do Drama as a separate subject in your school, you will know that a good deal of your work is based on improvisation: making it up as you go along, talking about what you are trying to do, reshaping your ideas and perhaps presenting your work to others. Perhaps a lot of your drama work is concerned with exploring a certain content – somebody's story, a theme or issue such as homelessness or teenage relationships.

● What sort of content do you find most interesting when you are making or watching drama?

There are some professional theatre companies who improvise all their own work and even some film directors who prefer their actors to improvise scenes around a basic idea. In most cases, though, the plays you see on stage and screen have, at some time or another in the process, been scripted, that is, the words that the characters say and some of the actions they perform have been written down.

This leads us to an extremely important point – scripts, with very few exceptions, are written to be performed.

● How many people in your class can read the following script?

It's the musical script for 'Happy Birthday to You'. It's easier to follow when you hear it played, isn't it? The same is true of playscripts – if you can't decode the signs the playwright is giving you it doesn't make much sense.

● Here is a different sort of example. What is it?

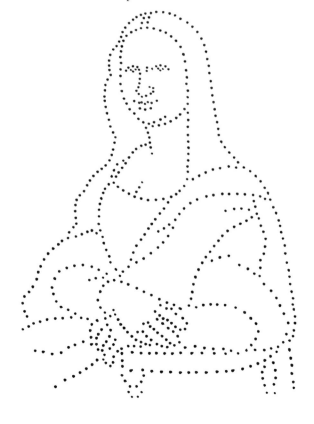

3

If you joined up all the dots correctly you would certainly get a picture. But would it look like this? If you think it would not, can you say why?

Just as joining the dots will not reproduce a great work of art, so simply saying the words printed on the page and following whatever stage directions are given will not result in a great production. The play will only come alive if the actors, directors and designers use their own talents to fill in the gaps, add something of their own and smooth over the rough edges. Every production of a play is different because those involved in it will be interpreting the words and actions of the script slightly differently. Any of you who have been involved in the production of a play will have noticed that every performance is slightly different. The audience on one night will laugh in different places from the night before, the show will seem to go faster than previously, perhaps different things will go wrong! Theatre is alive, ever changing, but the scripts on which most plays are built stay the same.

The purpose of the work in this book is to help you understand how playwrights give us clues about how to bring their plays to life. We hope that this will make reading and watching whole plays easier and more interesting for you. We also hope that it will help you make your own plays – whether improvised or written – far more interesting as you incorporate more and more of the tricks of the playwright's trade.

Novels

When you read a really good novel, it's as if you are drawn into the world of the characters. Perhaps you see in your 'mind's eye' what they are seeing. The writer can help you do this by using detailed description of places and what people look like. We can often gain a very clear understanding of why the characters do what they do because the author can tell us exactly what the characters are actually thinking. Writers can see into the minds of the characters and tell us, the readers, about what's going on in there – of course they can: they invented those characters!

● Read this example from a novel and talk about how successful the author has been in creating a clear picture in your mind of the character of the girl who is telling the story, her brother and the girl he is in love with.

My brother punches arms and makes remarks about smells like the rest of them, but he has a secret. He would never tell it to these other boys, because of the way they would laugh.

The secret is that he has a girlfriend. This girlfriend is so secret that she doesn't even know about it herself. I'm the only one he's told, and I have   5
been double-sworn not to tell anyone else. Even when we're alone I'm not allowed to refer to her by her name, only by her initials, which are B.W. My brother will sometimes murmur these initials when there are other people around, my parents for instance. When he says them he stares at me, waiting for me to nod or give some sign that I have heard and understood. He 10
writes me notes in code, which he leaves where I'll find them, under my pillow, tucked into my top bureau drawer. When I translate these notes they turn out to be so unlike him, so lacking in invention, so moronic in fact, that I can hardly believe it: 'Talked to B.W.' 'Saw HER today.' He writes these notes in coloured pencil, different colours, with exclamation 15
marks.

I can see that this girlfriend is causing him some anguish, as well as excitement, but I can't understand why. I know who she is. Her real name in Bertha Watson. She hangs around with the older girls, up on the hill under

the stunted fir trees. She has straight brown hair and she's of ordinary size. 20
There's no magic about her that I can see, or any abnormality. I'd like to
know how she's done it, this trick with my brother that's turned him into a
stupider, more nervous identical twin of himself.

adapted from *Cat's Eye* by Margaret Atwood

In most novels, the characters speak to each other. Some novels, like *Cat's
Eye*, are written in a way that makes us believe that one of the characters
actually wrote the story (we say that books like this are written in the **first person**). Because novels can give descriptions of where the story is happening and
what the characters are thinking, we are able to spot when those characters
aren't telling the whole truth to each other. We also notice when there is a difference between what they are thinking and what they are saying.

● Read through this extract and talk about how we know that what the character is actually saying isn't all of what they are thinking or feeling. What does this
tell us about the different characters in this passage?

If you really want to hear about it, the first thing you'll probably want to know
is where I was born, and what my lousy childhood was like, and how my
parents were occupied and all before they had me, and all that David
Copperfield kind of crap, but I don't feel like going into it. In the first place,
that stuff bores me, and in the second place, my parents would have about   5
two haemorrhages apiece if I told anything pretty personal about them.
They're quite touchy about anything like that, especially my father. They're
nice and all – I'm not saying that – but they're also touchy as hell. Besides,
I'm not going to tell you my whole goddam autobiography or anything. I'll
just tell you about this madman stuff that happened to me around last   10
Christmas before I got pretty run down and had to come out here and take
it easy. I mean that's all I told D.B. about, and he's my *brother* and all. He's
in Hollywood. That isn't too far from this crumby place, and he comes over
and visits me practically every week-end. He's going to drive me home when
I go home next month maybe. He just got a Jaguar. One of those little English   15
jobs that can do around two hundred miles an hour. It cost him damn near
four thousand bucks. He's got a lot of dough now. He didn't *use* to. He used
to be just a regular writer, when he was home. He wrote this terrific book of
short stories, *The Secret Goldfish*, in case you never heard of him. The best
one in it was 'The Secret Goldfish'. It was about this little kid that wouldn't   20

let anybody look at his goldfish because he'd bought it with his own money.
It killed me.

from *The Catcher in the Rye* by J.D. Salinger

When you watch a drama on television or at the cinema or on stage, you can
also see where the story is taking place and what people look like. You often tell
what they are thinking by the expression on their faces or the way they move
and respond to each other. You don't need to open the eye in your mind to imagine all this because there it is, on the screen or stage right in front of you.

The problem is, when you read the script of a play, you haven't got much to
go on to help you imagine all this. There are usually some **stage directions** to
help you get a picture of where the scene is set and what the characters are like,
but most of the words in a script are what the characters are actually saying.

The job of actors, directors and designers is to dig beneath what characters say
and make it clear to the audience why they might be saying it, and to help the
audience understand more about the situation.

When you read a novel you are the audience. The writer is talking directly to
you, telling you all you need to know to make up your own mind about the characters and the story. When you read a play, however, you must imagine that the
writer is talking to you as if you are an actor, director or designer. The writer will
be relying on those who read the play to make the story clear to an audience who
will watch the play when it is performed. When you read a play, you need to be
asking yourself not just *what* is happening, but *how* this will happen when the
play is produced.

● Read these two extracts. One is from the novel *Of Mice and Men*, the other
from a play based on that novel. Both were written by John Steinbeck.

She took Lenny's hand and put it on her head. 'Feel right aroun' there an'
see how soft it is.'

Lennie's big fingers fell to stroking her hair.

'Don't you muss it up,' she said.

Lennie said: 'Oh! That's nice,' and he stroked harder. 'Oh, that's nice.'   5

'Look out, now, you'll muss it.' And then she cried angrily: 'You stop it
now, you'll mess it all up.' She jerked her head sideways, and Lennie's fingers
closed on her hair and hung on. 'Let go,' she cried. 'You let go.'

Lennie was in a panic. His face contorted. She screamed then, and
Lennie's other hand closed over her mouth and nose.   10

'Please don't,' he begged. 'Oh! Please don't do that. George'll be mad.'

She struggled violently under his hands. Her feet battered on the hay and she writhed to be free; and from under Lennie's hand came a muffled scream- ing. Lennie began to cry with fright. 'Oh! Please don't do none of that,' he begged. 'George gonna say I done a bad thing. He ain't gonna let me tend no 15 rabbits.' He moved his hand a little and her hoarse cry came out. Then Lennie grew angry. 'Now don't,' he said. 'I don't want you to yell. You gonna get me in trouble jus' like George says you will. Now don't you do that.' And she con- tinued to struggle, and her eyes were wild with terror. He shook her then, and he was angry with her. 'Don't you go yellin',' he said, and he shook her; and 20 her body flopped like a fish. And then she was still, for Lennie had broken her neck.

CURLEY'S WIFE   [*She takes* LENNIE'*s hand and puts it on her head.*] Feel there and see how soft it is. [LENNIE'*s fingers fall to stroking her hair.*] Don't you muss it up.

LENNIE   Oh, that's nice. [*Strokes harder.*] Oh, that's nice.

CURLEY'S WIFE   Look out now, you'll muss it. [*Angrily.*] You stop it   5 now, you'll mess it all up. [*She jerks her head sideways and* LENNIE'*s fingers close on her hair and hang on. In a panic.*] Let go. [*She screams.*] You let go. [*She screams again. His other hand closes over her mouth and nose.*]

LENNIE   [*Begging.*] Oh, please don't do that. George'll be mad. [*She*   10 *struggles violently to be free. A soft screaming comes from under* LENNIE'*s hand. She is crying with fright.*] Oh, please don't do none of that. George gonna say I done a bad thing. [*He raises his hand from her mouth and a hoarse cry escapes. Angrily.*] Now don't. I don't want you to yell. You gonna get me in trouble just like George says you will.   15 Now don't you do that. [*She struggles more.*] Don't you go yellin'. [*He shakes her violently. Her neck snaps sideways and she lies still. He looks down at her and cautiously removes his hand from over her mouth.*]

● Make a note of three differences between the way the story is told in each extract.

● Now give two examples which show that the author is talking directly to the reader in the novel, but in the play he is telling the actors what to do.

● Read the novel extract through again to yourself and time how long it takes. Now read through the play extract. Imagine it happening on stage. How long do you think the scene would take in a performance? Can you explain why one might take longer than the other?

● Try performing the play extract, and experiment with speed/tempo, especially the early part up to 'Look out now, you'll muss it.' Which is more effective, a very fast treatment or very slow, or a subtle variation of the two?

Don't forget that when you are reading the novel this incident can happen as quickly or as slowly as you like, but if you are in the theatre audience these decisions have been made for you.

Unit 2   Reading for story

Some playwrights very generously tell us what the story is about before the play really starts. Even if they don't tell us exactly how the story will unfold, they give us lots of clues as to the type of play we are about to see and what the main action is likely to be.
● Read this extract, then answer the questions on it. It is from Ben Payne's play *The Last Laugh*.

_____

The cell

The glare from a single bulb lights the first page of a large open book. A voice is heard.

THE BOOK   This book has lain here long in jail
             Since its pages told an untrue tale
             Of a land, once upon a time,
             Where laughter once was made a crime.
             It's sad, cold folk lived deep in fear   5
             Beyond its grey and grim frontier.
             A line dividing right from wrong
             Two guards had guarded hard and long.
             Dogged lads, obeying orders
             Getting boreder, boreder on the border.   10

The page magically turns.

_____

● Do you think that this play is going to be entirely serious, or will there be something comical about it? What clues are there here which will help you decide how it should be played?

● Is there anything you notice about the way this introduction is written, including the stage directions, which remind you of other stories or perhaps films you know? Does that suggest anything about what the rest of the play might be like?

● Jot down, in just one or two sentences of your own, what the situation is at the start of this play.

● Now write down what you think is going to happen in this country where laughter has been banned (the fact that the play starts on the border of the country should give you a pretty good clue).

This way of opening a play is called a **prologue**. It's a technique used by many writers. In some ways, it's a bit like reading the description of a film in a television guide: both are written so that an audience can sit back and watch the story unfold without having to work too hard figuring out who is who and what is going on.

● Look at these cuttings from the *Radio Times* and compare them with the prologue from Shakespeare's *Romeo and Juliet*.

DRAMA
The X Files
9.30pm BBC1

An abduction that, for once, doesn't involve aliens is at the heart of this episode. Lucy Householder – who was kidnapped at the age of eight and held for five years in a basement – experiences a psychic connection with Amy, a missing teenager. At the exact moment Amy is abducted, Lucy uttered the same words spoken by the kidnapper before suffering a seizure and a nosebleed.

However, she insists that she can't help locate the missing girl because her psychic visions of Amy's situation are so terrifying. What will change her mind?

DRAMA
Wilderness
9.00pm ITV

By the concluding episode of this three-part drama, at least one person is beginning to accept Alice's bizarre assertion that once a month she turns into a wolf. Psychotherapist Luther finally admits that he believes the wolf is real but his obsession with this strange client may lead to his downfall. Meanwhile Alice's relationship with boyfriend Dan is as turbulent as ever, and her passionate and jealous feelings manifest themselves in a vicious attack by her wolf.

DRAMA
Dangerfield
9.30pm BBC1

Paul Dangerfield's personal life takes a back seat this week as he gets involved in a very complicated mystery involving an apparent suicide pact. He is called out early one morning to examine the body of a young woman found floating in a disused reservoir. Nearby are the remnants of a picnic and a man's distinctive red jacket. Soon afterwards, Dangerfield is consulted by another young woman, Beverley Groves, who is distressed because she suspects that her husband is having an affair. When she lets slip that he recently bought a red jacket, Dangerfield thinks the mystery is solved. Far from it.

DRAMA
Deadly Voyage
9.30pm BBC2

For the second time tonight, illegal immigration is the topic with this chilling *Screen Two* action film based on a true story. A lottery win encourages Kingsley, a young Ghanaian docker, to pursue his dream of becoming an engineer. With funds to make a start in America, he organises a group of friends to stowaway on a freighter bound for the west.

Unfortunately, the vessel is a rustbucket crewed by impoverished Ukrainians in fear of losing their livelihoods, and the crew's desperation to prevent any trouble with their employers leads to horrifying inhumanity.

Made for television with a budget larger than most British feature films, this is a gripping, thought-provoking drama. It stars up and coming American actor Omar Epps as Kingsley, with Joss Ackland, Sean Pertwee and David Suchet.

CHORUS   Two households, both alike in dignity
             In fair Verona, where we lay our scene,
             From ancient grudge break to new mutiny,
             Where civil blood makes civil hands unclean.
             From forth the fatal loins of these two foes   5
             A pair of star-crossed lovers take their life.

                                          from *Romeo and Juliet*

11

● Rewrite Shakespeare's prologue to make it more like the snippets from the *Radio Times*. Say:

   Where the story takes place
   Who the story is mainly about
   What their problem is
   What happens in the end.

Unit 3   The plot

If the prologue tells you what happens in the play, you might be wondering what the point of reading or watching the whole thing is! The simple answer is that although we know from the prologue that Romeo and Juliet die, we haven't been told how it all happened – what the **plot** is (that is, the sequence of events which make up the story).

One way of discovering the plot of a play quite quickly is for everyone in the class to read just a small section or scene each. Even if you don't understand what everyone is saying and why, you will be able to pick out the main event – the key thing that happens in that scene.

In *Romeo and Juliet* there are a total of 24 scenes. By picking out the main events from each scene, the plot could be summarised like this:

◆ Two families live in Verona. They are called the Montagues and the Capulets. They have been arguing for years.

◆ After a fight in the street, the Prince tells Montague and Capulet that if there is any more trouble he will punish the wrongdoers by death.

◆ Montague has a son called Romeo. He is in love with a girl called Rosaline and decides to gate-crash a party at the Capulets' house in order to see her.

◆ At the party, Capulet gives Paris permission to woo their daughter who is called Juliet.

◆ Romeo and Juliet meet at the party and instantly fall in love.

◆ Tybalt, a nephew of Capulet, spots Romeo and is angered by his presence at the party.

◆ Romeo jumps over Capulet's wall and hears Juliet talking about how much she loves him.

◆ He reveals himself to her and they agree to get married as soon as possible.

◆ Romeo goes to Friar Lawrence who agrees to marry them in secret.

◆ Tybalt threatens Romeo in the street but Romeo doesn't want to fight him.

◆ Romeo's friend Mercutio gets involved and is killed by Tybalt.

◆ Romeo kills Tybalt in revenge.

◆ Romeo hides in Friar Lawrence's cell and is told that the Prince has banished him.

◆ Juliet is upset when she hears that Romeo has been banished. Her parents think that she is grieving for Tybalt. They tell her she should marry Paris as soon as possible.

◆ Juliet's Nurse and Friar Lawrence help her marry Romeo and they spend the night together.

◆ In the morning Romeo escapes.

◆ Juliet refuses to marry Paris. Her parents are angry.

◆ Friar Lawrence suggests that she should take a powerful sleeping drug which will make her appear dead in order to get out of marrying Paris.

◆ Friar Lawrence sends a letter to Romeo (who has now fled to another town) telling him to rescue Juliet from the Capulets' tomb.

◆ Juliet takes the potion and appears to die.

◆ Friar Lawrence's letter does not arrive but Romeo does hear that Juliet is dead.

◆ Romeo buys a poison and returns to Verona.

◆ While he is breaking into the Capulets' tomb he is caught by Paris. They fight and Paris is killed.

◆ Romeo sees Juliet, thinks that she is really dead, and poisons himself.

◆ Juliet wakes up. She sees the dead Romeo, and stabs herself with his dagger.

◆ Friar Lawrence arrives along with the Prince and the Capulets. Montague arrives and says his wife has died of grief.

◆ The Prince declares that the feud must now stop.

─────────────

● To make the plot clearer, try just acting out this summary in the simplest way. You will need:

4 long blue ribbons for Romeo, Montague, Lady Montague and Friar Lawrence.

5 long yellow ribbons for Juliet, Capulet, Lady Capulet, Tybalt and the Nurse.

3 long white ribbons for the Prince, Mercutio and Paris.
6 long black ribbons for all the people who die!

● Clear a space in the classroom and stand around it in a horseshoe shape. One person should slowly read through the summary printed above. As each new character is mentioned, a volunteer is given the appropriately coloured ribbon to hang around their neck. They enter the space and adopt a pose which fits that part of the story. Whenever somebody is killed, they hang a black ribbon around their neck and then stand on a chair at the back of the playing space.

By using this technique, the main part of the story is shown just through still images and becomes much easier to remember than the words alone. By trying out the exercise, you will have taken the first steps that actors and directors take when they are **blocking** a play. Blocking is a word we use to describe the way in which actors and directors decide who is going to stand where and when they need to move.

● Having run through the whole story in still images and with a narrator, you might like to try this again, only this time improvise a few lines and actions which you think would fit each part of the story.

Unit 4   Setting the scene

Another obvious difference between a play and a novel is the way the reader or audience comes to know who the story is about and where the story is taking place. Many novels seem to start in the middle of a story and the reader must go on some way before she discovers not only what is happening but where the action is taking place.

● Choose any two novels and read through the first two pages of each. Compare the way they open and make notes on the following questions:

Who is telling the story?
Who does the story seem to be about?
How much do we know about where the story takes place?

When you read a play, one of the first things you will encounter will be the cast list or **dramatis personae**. This tells you immediately what characters appear in the play. Similarly, when you buy a programme at the theatre, all of the character names are listed along with the actors who will be playing them. You may think that listing the characters like this takes away an element of surprise but the fact that cast lists are printed tells us something important about how to read a play.

● Why do you think it may be useful to have a cast list at the beginning of a published play? Who needs it?

• Why do audiences in the theatre want to see a cast list in the programme? Is it important to know which actors are playing which parts?

Once the lights go down in the **auditorium** and the curtain is opened on the stage, the audience will be able to see immediately where the first scene of the play is to take place because of the setting. In the printed version of the play the audience's first experience is often captured in a description of the **set**. For example:

A winter evening in Holmes' sitting-room in Baker Street.

It's a comfortable Victorian room, with a coal fire burning in the grate, two armchairs, a table set for supper, a desk with a chair, and a sofa which is partly concealed from the audience by a folding screen. The walls are lined with bookshelves, and every surface seems to be cluttered with papers, chemical apparatus, racks of tobacco-pipes, soda syphons, Holmes' violin . . . a Persian slipper is hanging next to the fire, and a jack-knife is stuck through a pile of letters on the mantelpiece.

There are two doors: one to the landing and the rest of the house, the other to Holmes' bedroom.

When we first see it, the room is lit only by the dim light coming through the half-drawn curtains.

from *Sherlock Holmes and the Limehouse Horror* by Philip Pullman

---

• From this description of Holmes' room, what do we immediately learn about the man and the period in which the story is set?
• If somebody was to write a play about you and set the first scene in your bedroom, what details do you think they should make sure appeared on the set which said something about your character? List ten things about your room that are very particular to you.
• Now invent a character of your own. They may come from any time or place. Write a brief description of a set, or sketch and label a diagram of it that would immediately tell an audience something important about the character.

Quite frequently nowadays, a curtain isn't used and the audience can view the **set** as they sit waiting for the play to start. Some plays are, of course, performed on a completely empty stage, or the playwright has decided to leave it to the **director** and **designer** to decide what the set should look like.

Lark Rise is a play written by Keith Dewhurst based on the novel *Lark Rise to Candleford* by Flora Thompson. This is how the play opens:

LAURA   The hamlet stood on a gentle rise in the flat, wheat-growing north-east corner of Oxfordshire. We will call it Lark Rise because of the great number of skylarks which made the surrounding fields their springboard and nested on the bare earth between the rows of green corn. For a few days or a week or a fortnight, the fields stood   5
'ripe unto harvest'. It was the one perfect period in the hamlet's year. The 1880s brought a succession of hot summers, and day after day, as harvest time approached, the children of the end house would wake to the dewy pearly pink of a fine summer dawn, and the swizzh, swizzh of the early morning breeze rustling through the ripe   10
corn beyond their doorstep ...

● Pick out all of the words or phrases in Laura's opening speech which help you to imagine what her hamlet looked like.
● Do you think it would be necessary to actually build the hamlet or show the fields on stage if you were to produce this play? How else might you help create an appropriate atmosphere for this play, given Laura's description?
● If you feel that some sort of set might be useful for the play *Lark Rise*, sketch a design for it.

Both *Sherlock Holmes and the Limehouse Horror* and *Lark Rise* seem to transport the audience back to another time and place. They set up the scene in a way that invites the audience to forget that they are in a theatre and just enjoy the story that will unfold before them. Other plays do the opposite. Read this extract from Tennessee Williams' play *The Glass Menagerie*:

TOM   Yes, I have tricks in my pocket, I have things up my sleeve. But I am the opposite of a stage magician. He gives you illusion that has the appearance of truth. I give you truth in the pleasant disguise of illusion.
To begin with, I turn back time ...   5

[*Music.*]

16

The play is memory.
Being a memory play, it is dimly lighted, it is sentimental, it is not realistic.
In memory everything seems to happen to music. That explains the fiddle in the wings.   10
I am the narrator of the play, and also a character in it.
The other characters are my mother Amanda, my sister Laura, and a gentleman caller who appears in the final scenes.
He is the most realistic character in the play, being an emissary from a world of reality that we were somehow set apart from.   15
But since I have a poet's weakness for symbols, I am using this character also as a symbol; he is the long-delayed but always expected something that we live for.
There is a fifth character in the play who doesn't appear except in this larger-than-life-size photograph over the mantel.   20
This is our father who left us a long time ago.
He was a telephone man who fell in love with long distances; he gave up his job with the telephone company and skipped the light fantastic out of town . . .
The last we heard of him was a picture postcard from Mazatlan, on   25
the Pacific coast of Mexico, containing a message of two words –
'Hello – Goodbye!' and no address.
I think the rest of the play will explain itself . . .

● This seems a very strange way to open a play, but perhaps quite an intriguing one. What important things about this play does the playwright seem to be telling you?

● Is there anything about this opening which would make you want to read on or see the rest of the play? Make a note of three questions which you would hope to have answered by the end of the play.

Unit 5   Special strategies

As you work through the units in this book you will come across a wide range of tricks that playwrights use to make their work lively. Many of these devices have special names and you will find an explanation of the terms in the glossary at the back of this book. Just to get you going on this, look up the following words in the glossary and ask yourself if you have ever seen these particular devices used in a play or film:

aside	stereotype	monologue	set
personification	SFX	anagnorisis	narration

Not too difficult really, are they?

In this unit you are going to focus on the last one of these terms, **narration**. It's a device with which you will no doubt already be very familiar (think of the primary school nativity play in which a child comes forward and says, 'Then the angel Gabriel came down to Mary and told her that she would have a very special baby').

Using a narrator can be an efficient way of telling the audience a part of the story. The trouble is it isn't very dramatic. Audiences prefer to see the action rather than be told about it; or at least, if they are going to just sit and listen then the narration somehow has to be made interesting.

● Read how playwright Brian Woolland gives us vital information at the start of his play *Gulliver*:

BETTY   But what about the beginning of it, father?

GULLIVER ONE *settles down to tell his story – which he greatly enjoys doing.*

GULLIVER ONE   Start at the beginning?

MARY   Do we have time?

GULLIVER ONE   I think Betty and Johnny want to hear it from the   5
beginning, don't you? [*But he doesn't give them time to respond.*] Very
well then, from the beginning: my father had a small estate in
Nottinghamshire. I was the third of five sons.

MARY   His father sent him to Emmanuel College at fourteen years old.

GULLIVER ONE   Where I resided three years and applied myself close   10
to my studies.

As GULLIVER ONE *tells his story a second Gulliver (dressed identically
and known as* GULLIVER TWO) *appears, along with all the other characters mentioned. They act out Gulliver's story.*

FATHER   But the charge of maintaining him

GULLIVER TWO   Although I had but a scant allowance

FATHER   Proved too great for his father's narrow fortune.

GULLIVER TWO   So I was bound apprentice   15

MR BATES   To Mister James Bates, an eminent surgeon in London.

GULLIVER TWO   With whom I continued four years,

FATHER   His father now and then sending him sums of money

GULLIVER ONE   *Small* sums of money.

GULLIVER TWO   I laid them out in navigation, and in other parts of the   20
Mathematics useful to those who intend to travel,

GULLIVER ONE   As I always believed it would, sometime or other, be
my fortune to do.

MR BATES   Mister Bates encouraged him to settle in London.

GULLIVER ONE   Being advised to alter my condition,   25

GULLIVER TWO   I married

MARY   Mistress Mary Burton

BURTON   Second daughter to Mr Edmund Burton, hosier in Newgate
Street,

GULLIVER ONE   From whom I received   30

BURTON   Four hundred pounds

MARY   As a dowry.

GULLIVER ONE   Having consulted my wife

GULLIVER TWO   and some of my acquaintances,

GULLIVER ONE   I determined to go to sea, accepting an advantageous   35
offer from

PRITCHARD   Captain William Pritchard, Master of the Antelope,
making a voyage to the South Sea . . .

And now MARY *becomes part of Gulliver's story.*

MARY   Will you write?

GULLIVER TWO   Of course.   40

● Try acting out this scene. You will need either eight characters or, and this could be interesting, a way of swopping the parts over between a smaller number of actors. The aim is to give the audience all the background information they need in a way that is clear, good to listen to and watch.

● You can experiment with this technique yourself by choosing a well-known fairy story. Stand in a line and face forward. Find a way of bouncing the story along the line, changing your voice and the way you stand as each new character enters; other characters in the line might act out or react to the action being described at any given moment. The trick is to keep facing forward and not actually look at each other but just tell *and show* the audience the story.

● Go back to the scene from *Gulliver*. Would this work as a 'line story', or could it be made more interesting by having the characters weaving in and out of each other as they play their part? Either way, we're sure you'll agree that this is rather more interesting than just having one actor telling the whole story.

Unit 6   Chorus

You already know that the word **chorus** can mean the refrain in a song, that is, the part that is repeated and perhaps everyone joins in. In a musical the chorus is the group of singers who sing the songs from the show, sometimes supporting the main characters but at other times singing a song which tells the audience what is happening or how one of the characters is feeling.

You might find a chorus in some plays also. The members of the chorus are in role but not as individuals. They set the scene and comment on the action. Their speech is often quite poetic and works to a pattern.

The beginnings of the chorus in Western drama are in the plays of the ancient Greeks. Originally, the chorus told the story without any actors at all but then plays began to appear with one individual actor (perhaps the Greeks too got fed up with just listening to the story!). This character was called the **protagonist**. He (yes, it was always a he) was the main person in the story and could react to what the chorus was saying. Soon the ball really got rolling and a second actor was introduced (called the **deuteragonist**) – now they could talk to each other (the excitement must have been unbearable!). Eventually they added the **tritagonist** – a third actor. We still use the word protagonist to describe the main character in a play.

The chorus could number between 15 and 50. They would sing and dance (a bit, and not in a way you would recognise now) so you can see how they resembled what we would call a chorus today.

In this extract from *Oedipus the King* by Sophocles, who wrote in the 5th century BC, you can see how the story is told by the chorus asking questions and one of the characters answering.

SERVANT   Rulers of Thebes, I've terrible news to bring you! Terrible to hear, terrible to see, and terrible to report.
CHORUS   What has happened?
SERVANT   A pollution so horrible, that all the rivers of Thebes will never wash it clean!   5
CHORUS   Could anything be worse than what we know already?
SERVANT   Yes, this! Jocasta the Queen is dead!
CHORUS   Dead? How?
SERVANT   By her own hand! I'll never forget the sight!
CHORUS   But how did it happen?   10

And if you think this news about the Queen is bad, wait till you hear what the servant has to say about the King!
● Improvise a continuation of this scene – you'll have to invent how the Queen died and possibly what the King did next. Remember, it's a chorus so you need several voices talking in unison. When you've had a go at this, talk about the dramatic effectiveness of what you've achieved or what you think could be achieved with enough rehearsal.

A particularly useful function of the chorus in this play is that the audience can be given really gruesome details of something that has happened that could be very difficult to actually show on stage. Violent scenes in Greek tragedies are always reported, not acted out in front of the audience. Shakespeare was quite happy to show acts of violence on stage, but he also used the device of the chorus for other purposes. He tended to have just one actor playing the chorus.
● In the following extract, which comes from a play called *Murder in the Cathedral* by the poet T.S. Eliot, the chorus sets the scene at the start of the play. What atmosphere do you think they manage to create?

CHORUS   Here let us stand, close by the cathedral. Here let us wait.
          Are we drawn by danger? Is it the knowledge of safety that
               draws our feet
          Towards the cathedral? What danger can there be
          For us, the poor, poor women of Canterbury? What tribulation
          With which we are not already familiar? There is no danger   5
          For us, and there is no safety in the cathedral. Some presage
               of an act
          Which our eyes are compelled to witness, has forced our feet
          Towards the cathedral. We are forced to bear witness.

Notice that the speech is in verse. There are patterns and repetitions in the words. What effect does this produce? At first the scene might appear static but if performed well it can be tremendously dramatic.

Sometimes characters fulfil what we might call a 'choric function'. This means that they are not really interesting individuals in their own right, but are used on stage to tell the audience what is going on. In the following example there are three woodcutters commenting on two lovers who have run away together. Do you think they will get very far?

W 1   Have they found them yet?
W 2   Not yet. But they'll not leave a single stone unturned.
W 3   They'll get them.
W 2   Sssh!
W 3   What?   5
W 2   They're closing round . . . along every path.
W 1   They'll see them as soon as the moon rises.
W 2   They should let them go.
W 1   The world is wide. There's room for everyone.
W 3   But they'll kill them.   10
W 2   They were right to run away . . . to take their own path.
W 1   They were just fooling themselves . . . until at last their blood
begin to simmer . . .
W 3   Blood.

from *Blood Wedding* by Federico García Lorca

● Pick out:
  those lines that set the atmosphere
  those lines that tell the audience what is happening elsewhere
  those lines that comment on the story.
● Try acting the scene out in different ways, for example:
  the woodcutters are gossiping over a fence
  they are placed at a distance from each other across the stage
  they stand in a line facing the audience.
● What different effects can you achieve by how you place them and the way
they use their voices?
● What do you think will happen to the lovers? And what will the woodcutters
say then? Devise a new piece of choral speech that reports what happened.

The last extract which shows a chorus at work comes from *My Mother Said I
Never Should* by Charlotte Keatley. It was written in 1988. The play is about four
different generations of mothers and daughters, but at the start of the play all
four characters appear as little girls playing together. The words they sing and say
are very familiar, but in this context they form a chorus which expresses one of
the central themes of the play: that is, how mothers influence, or try to influence, their daughters.

Act One Scene One

A patch of wasteground at the end of a terraced street, where children play.
Four girls enter, each dressed contemporary to her own generation. They hold
hands and spin round fast, singing.

> My mother said I never should
> Play with the gypsies in the wood,
> If I did, she would say,
> Naughty girl to disobey!

They split off from the circle. JACKIE *watches the others.*

ROSIE [*chanting*]   What are little girls made of? [*Coaxing* DORIS *to*   5
answer.] Ssh . . .
DORIS   Sugar – and – [*Effort.*] spice . . .?
MARGARET   And . . .
DORIS   [*Desperately stuck.*] And?
MARGARET   All things nice.   10

DORIS, squirming, doesn't want to repeat it.

● Try acting out this scene. Make sure you follow the stage directions carefully.
The words that the little girls say seem innocent enough but, when you stage it,
what atmosphere seems to be generated?

Unit 7   Dramatic irony

The chorus, or a character functioning as a chorus, is used to put the audience
in the picture – and that's one of the great joys of plays, knowing what is going
on! It's even better if *we* know what's going on but the characters in the play
don't. The term for this is **dramatic irony.**

In this section you will look in detail at just one example. It is from a play
called *The Rivals* which was written by Richard Brinsley Sheridan in 1775.
Sheridan was critical of the number of 'sentimental comedies' which were being
performed at the time and more interested in showing how silly people could be.
If you have seen any of the recent film or television adaptations of Jane Austen's
novels you will have a good idea of the period in which the play is set. Like

Sheridan, Jane Austen was amused by the antics of people, especially when they were in love. Life at that time was very 'mannered'; there was a 'correct' way of doing just about everything if you wanted to be accepted into 'polite' society. Because people couldn't always say or do what they really wanted openly they could get themselves into terrible tangles, and some writers at the time were quick to exploit this to make people, and indeed the whole 'mannered' society, look a bit ridiculous. A skill that came in particularly handy for surviving this sort of society was wit. Having a quick brain and a sharp tongue would allow you to get what you wanted without appearing rude.

Sheridan was famous for his wit both as a playwright and as a politician. One evening he was called from the House of Commons to watch the Drury Lane Theatre, which he owned, burn down. As he stood watching it he drank a glass of wine, and when asked why he was doing this he replied, 'Is a man not allowed to take a glass by his own fireside?'

Something you must remember whenever you are reading a play is that *the characters are not real!* People in plays simply don't behave like real people. An audience is sometimes given the illusion that they are watching real people, but of course everything that is said or done on stage in a play has been worked out beforehand with the intention of telling a story and making a point. Sometimes, as in *The Rivals*, this **conceit** (conceit can mean 'a fanciful notion' as well as referring to someone who is big headed) is very obvious, but no one cares because they know they are watching a comedy rather than a documentary.

Look at the conceit at work in the following scene. Before you read the scene, here's a summary of the story so far:

Lydia Languish is Mrs Malaprop's niece. She wants to marry a poor army officer for love rather than money. Captain Absolute, who is in fact very rich, knows this so disguises himself as the poorly paid Ensign Beverley and wins her love. The snag is, if she marries without the consent of her aunt she will lose half her fortune. Mrs Malaprop forbids her to see Ensign Beverley, so they have to write to each other secretly. In the meantime, Captain Absolute's father and Mrs Malaprop have planned together that Lydia should marry Captain Absolute (who Lydia refuses to see because he is rich). Absolute then is in a bit of a pickle. He decides to go and see Mrs Malaprop in order to try and get to Lydia to explain that he is the same Ensign Beverley that she loves.

With it so far? Now read the scene:

MRS MALAPROP   I thought she had persisted from corresponding with him; but behold this very day, I have interceded another letter from the fellow! I have it in my pocket.

ABSOLUTE [*Aside.*]   O the devil! my last note.

MRS MALAPROP   Aye, here it is.   5

ABSOLUTE [*Aside.*]   Aye, my note indeed!

MRS MALAPROP   There, perhaps you know the writing.

[*Gives him the letter.*]

ABSOLUTE   I think I have seen the hand before – yes, I certainly must have seen this hand before –

MRS MALAPROP   Nay, but read it, Captain.   10

ABSOLUTE [*Reads.*]   *My soul's idol, my adored Lydia!* Very tender indeed!

MRS MALAPROP   Tender! aye, and profane too, o' my conscience!

ABSOLUTE   *I am excessively alarmed at the intelligence you send me, the more so as my new rival –*   15

MRS MALAPROP   That's you, Sir.

ABSOLUTE   *has universally the character of being an accomplished gentleman, and a man of honour.* Well, that's handsome enough.

MRS MALAPROP   Oh, the fellow had some design in writing so –

ABSOLUTE   That he had, I'll answer for him, Ma'am.   20

MRS MALAPROP   But go on, Sir – you'll see presently.

ABSOLUTE   *As for the old weather-beaten, she-dragon who guards you –* who can he mean by that?

MRS MALAPROP   *Me,* Sir – *me* – he means *me* there – what do you think now? But go on a little further.   25

ABSOLUTE   Impudent scoundrel! – *it shall go hard but I will elude her vigilance, as I am told that the same ridiculous vanity, which makes her dress up her coarse features, and deck her dull chat with hard words which she don't understand –*

MRS MALAPROP   There, Sir! an attack upon my language! what do   30
you think of that? An aspersion upon my parts of speech! Was ever such a brute! Sure if I reprehend anything in this world, it is the use of my oracular tongue, and a nice derangement of epitaphs!

ABSOLUTE   He deserves to be hanged and quartered! let me see – *same*   35
ridiculous vanity –

MRS MALAPROP   You need not read it again, Sir.

ABSOLUTE   I beg pardon, Ma'am – *does also lay her open to the grossest deceptions from flattery and pretended admiration* – an impudent coxcomb! – *so that I have a scheme to see you shortly with the old harridan's consent, and even to make her a go-between in our interviews.* – Was ever such assurance?   40

MRS MALAPROP   Did you ever hear anything like it? He'll elude my vigilance, will he? Yes, yes! ha! ha! He's very likely to enter these doors! We'll try who can plot best.   45

ABSOLUTE   So we will Ma'am – so we will. Ha! ha! ha! a conceited puppy, ha! ha! ha! Well, but Mrs Malaprop, as the girl seems so infatuated by this fellow, suppose you were to wink at her corresponding with him for a little time – let her even plot an elopement with him – then do you connive at her escape – while *I*, just in the   50 nick, will have the fellow laid by the heels, and fairly contrive to carry her off in his stead.

MRS MALAPROP   I am delighted with the scheme, never was anything better perpetrated!

ABSOLUTE   But, pray, could not I see the lady for a few minutes now?   55 I should like to try her temper a little.

MRS MALAPROP   Why, I don't know – I doubt she is not prepared for a visit of this kind. There is a decorum in these matters.

ABSOLUTE   O Lord! She won't mind *me* – only tell her Beverley –

MRS MALAPROP   Sir!   60

ABSOLUTE [*Aside.*]   Gently, good tongue.

MRS MALAPROP   What did you say of Beverley?

ABSOLUTE   Oh, I was going to propose that you should tell her, by way of jest, that it was Beverley who was below – she'd come down fast enough then – ha! ha! ha!   65

MRS MALAPROP   'Twould be a trick she well deserves – besides you know the fellow tells her he'll get my consent to see her – ha! ha! Let him if he can, I say again. [*Calling.*] Lydia, come down here! He'll make me a go-between in their interviews! – ha! ha! ha!   70

- Read the scene through once more then make brief notes on:
  What Ensign Beverley, who wrote the letter, thinks of Mrs Malaprop.
  What Mrs Malaprop appears to think about herself.
  How Captain Absolute wants to appear in Mrs Malaprop's eyes.
- Pick out all the places in the script where the theatre audience is being invited

to laugh because they know something that Mrs Malaprop doesn't. For example, Absolute says that he thinks he recognises the handwriting – not surprising, of course, because it is his own!

● Now, remembering that Captain Absolute and Ensign Beverley are one and the same person, how could the actor playing the part hide this fact from Mrs Malaprop yet remind the audience of the truth? In pairs, try to stage this extract imagining that there is an audience watching who are already in on the conceit. In comedies like *The Rivals* dramatic irony is used as a way of making the audience part of an in-joke. We can have a laugh at Mrs Malaprop when she confidently says that there will be no way for Ensign Beverley to get into her house and use her as a go-between when in fact he is standing right in front of her and using her in exactly this way.

● Improvise another scene that might appear in *The Rivals* which could use dramatic irony. For example:

Mrs Malaprop telling Lydia how nice Captain Absolute is in comparison to the dreadful Ensign Beverley after Lydia has discovered that they are one and the same;

Captain Absolute's father trying to persuade his son to challenge Beverley to a duel.

● You might, of course, consider what happens in the scene after the one printed here in which Lydia enters determined not even to look at Absolute because she despises her aunt choosing her husband.

In serious plays, dramatic irony can be used for a very different effect. Imagine, for example, that it has been left to a neighbour to tell a woman that her child has been killed in an accident. Breaking the news is made more difficult because when the woman enters she is in a particularly jolly mood – perhaps she has just managed to buy a really jokey present for the child's birthday.

● Make up a scene of your own along these lines. Experiment with ways of building the tension in order to give the scene more impact when the truth is finally revealed.

An extreme case!

Dramatic irony can take many forms. One of the most extreme examples is Peter Shaffer's play *Black Comedy*. In many ways this is a typical situation comedy involving people meeting for a little social gathering in which there are some tricky personal relations. What makes the play very funny for the audience, though, is that the play starts in complete darkness: we can hear the people speaking normally and are perhaps wondering if there has been some technical problem with the theatre's lighting. Suddenly all the lights come up on stage though we hear from the characters that there has been a power cut! For the rest of the play the characters grope around the room (and each other) as if they are in complete darkness, while the audience can see everything that is going on. The idea is well worth experimenting with in groups of your own (for the purposes of understanding how dramatic irony works, of course, rather than just fulfilling any of your own personal desires!).

Section two   The Language of plays

Section summary

8   *Voicing the lines*

The focus of this unit is on encouraging the students to move on from simply reading the play aloud to playing with the sounds of the words in order to see how tone and volume, for example, can change the meaning of the text. Extracts from *Romeo and Juliet*, *The Tempest*, Willis Hall's *Billy Liar* and *Much Ado About Nothing* are used. The emphasis on Shakespeare is deliberate as it is with his plays that students most commonly find the language a barrier to their enjoyment and understanding.

9   *Dialogue*

This unit gives students an opportunity to create their own short dramatic dialogues. Extracts from Harold Pinter's *The Birthday Party*, Caryl Churchill's *Three More Sleepless Nights*, Tom Stoppard's *The Real Inspector Hound* and Mary Morris' *Two Weeks With the Queen* are used to explore the way in which playwrights use dialogue to give essential information to the audience.

10   *And now for the news . . .*

The exercises here aim to show students that there are alternatives to dialogue in dramatic writing. Short extracts from *Oh What a Lovely War*, *Touched* by Stephen Lowe and *Anansi* by Alistair Campbell suggest some of these other forms.

11   *Direct address*

This unit is closely linked with the preceding one and explores conventions such as the aside, monologue and soliloquy as other forms of dramatic writing. Extracts from *Moll Flanders* by Claire Luckham, *He Who Says Yes* by Bertolt Brecht, *Drink the Mercury* by Belgrade TIE Co., *Indians* by Arthur Kopit and *Oh What a Lovely War* by Theatre Workshop form the basis of the unit.

12   *Rhythm*

Teachers might find it useful to use these exercises in conjunction with the unit 'Voicing the lines'. An extract from Lin Coghlan's play *A Feeling in My Bones* leads onto an exploration of the deliberate use of poetry in plays, where a sonnet from *Romeo and Juliet* is offered for practical work.

13   Rhythm in conversation

This unit is a natural follow on from the previous one but may also be used independently. Extracts from Harold Pinter's *The Birthday Party* and Forkbeard Fantasy's *Work Ethic* offer a contrast of how playwrights try to either capture the natural rhythms of speech or deliberately create unnatural rhythms for theatrical effect. This leads onto an exploration of stichomythia where an extract from *The Taming of the Shrew* is compared to another piece from *The Birthday Party*.

14   What's my line?

This is the first of four units which could be used independently of each other but might be useful to use in sequence. In this unit, students are asked to think about the way lines are individual to characters by matching a selection of lines to character names.

15   First impressions

The work introduced here is developed further in the section 'Experiencing the production'. It encourages the students to assess how their expectations of a play are shaped in the first instance.

16   Moody moments

Extracts from J.R. Planche's *The Vampire*, Chris Bond's *The Blood of Dracula* and Martin Sherman's *Bent* are used to give an introduction to genre . . .

17   Genre

. . . which is further explored through extracts from *Kidnapped at Christmas* by Willis Hall, *The Deep Blue Sea* by Terence Rattigan and *Journey's End* by R.C. Sherrif.

18   Style

This unit is offered as an extension to the preceding one. The difference between style and genre is explained and explored through extracts from *The Dumb Waiter* and *The Room* by Harold Pinter and *Waiting for Godot* by Samuel Beckett.

19   Positioning the audience

Extracts from *Example* by the Belgrade TIE Co. and *Bartholomew Fair* by Ben Jonson explore how an audience is explicitly told what to expect from the play.

20   Playing with the illusion

This is an extension of the preceding unit; it looks at more sophisticated devices for using the unreality of the theatre as a means of creating dramatic effect. Extracts from Peter Nichols' *A Day in the Death of Joe Egg*, Tom Stoppard's *Rosencrantz and Guildenstern Are Dead* and *Waiting for Godot* by Samuel Beckett are used as examples.

21   Stage, screen and radio

The previous units have all focused on writing for the stage but this one serves as an introduction to how writing for other media presents different opportunities and challenges for the writer and indeed the reader. Extracts from the stage and screen versions of *Shakers* and Cara May's radio play *First Come, First Served* are presented along with samples of Martin Scorsese's storyboard for the film *Raging Bull*. Finally, a piece of writing by Roger McGough gives students the chance of playing with radio sound effects themselves.

Unit 8   Voicing the lines

What insults would you throw at someone from a rival gang? More to the point, how exactly would you say them?

● Share some of your favourite insults and put downs with the rest of the class. Score a point for any you have that no one else has, but lose a point for any which are obscene!

● Here are some of the insults Shakespeare wrote for the characters in his play *Romeo and Juliet*:

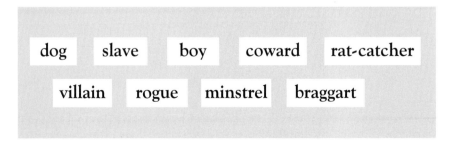

dog   slave   boy   coward   rat-catcher

villain   rogue   minstrel   braggart

31

Pretty harmless by today's standards, perhaps, but can you make them sound like heartfelt insults?
● Find a partner, and stand or sit as far away from each other as possible. Use these words to insult each other. How can you use your face and your tone of voice to really make it sound as if you hate each other?
● Working in pairs, imagine that you are rivals who have come face to face in a disco. Rehearse this piece of dialogue. Try it a few times in different ways – loudly, quietly, quickly, with lots of pauses.

Are you staring at me?
I'm just staring.
I said, are you staring at me?
I'm staring at nothing.
You looking for a fight?   5
With you?

In Italy, where *Romeo and Juliet* was set, it was considered a great insult to flick your top front teeth with your thumb in someone's direction – it was the equivalent of sticking two fingers up at them – not very nice and very likely to get you into a fight!
● Form two lines, with each member of the class facing their partner. Start quite close together, then move further apart as you speak these lines to each other. When you get to the end of the sequence just start over again. As before, experiment with using different volume and tone to see which is most effective. (It would help this exercise a great deal if you actually learnt these lines, then you could try to outstare each other as you said them!)

Do you bite your thumb at us, sir?
I do bite my thumb, sir.
Do you bite your thumb at us, sir?
No, sir, I do not bite my thumb at you, sir. But I bite my thumb, sir.
Do you quarrel, sir?   5
Quarrel, sir! No, sir.

Usually, when we call someone 'sir' it is because we respect them or are a bit frightened of them. Do you think the word 'sir' is being used here because the

speakers respect each other? How can you say 'sir' and yet make it sound like an insult?
● Repeat the exercise above, but when you get to the end of Shakespeare's lines, start to use some of your own invention. The intention is to give the impression that at any moment a huge fight is going to erupt – but you won't actually get that far!

For goodness sake, BE QUIET!

We've all been in the situation when a class without a teacher goes a bit mad. Suddenly, a teacher walks into the riot. What do they say over the noise?
● Write a short speech that a teacher might make to try to get some order back into the class. You will need to imagine that when they first enter nobody notices!

In *Romeo and Juliet* the Prince has the same problem. Just as the fight is about to really get going he enters and warns them of the trouble they will be in unless they calm down.
● Look at the punctuation in this speech and note Shakespeare's use of alliteration (all those 'p's) to show the trouble the Prince is having being heard and how angry he is.

PRINCE   Rebellious subjects, enemies to peace,
          Profaners of this neighbour-stained steel –
          Will they not hear? What ho – you men, you beasts,
          That quench the fire of your pernicious rage
          With purple fountains issuing from your veins!   5
          On pain of torture, from those bloody hands
          Throw your mistemper'd weapons to the ground
          And hear the sentence of your moved prince.

● Set up the quarrel as you did above, but this time have one member of the class (the one with the loudest voice perhaps!) enter into the middle and try to get the attention of everyone just by speaking the Prince's lines.

What did you say?

'The hardest thing about trying to read Shakespeare's plays is the language.'
    That's a very common remark, but what does it mean? Certainly, Shakespeare

uses quite a lot of words that you might be unfamiliar with. Just what is a 'pernicious rage', what are 'profaners'? How can a weapon be 'mistempered'?

Apart from the actual words he used, Shakespeare tended to phrase his lines in a way that is now quite unfamiliar to us. This is partly because people in England 400 years ago spoke differently anyway, and partly because Shakespeare deliberately tried to put certain rhythms into his plays – something we will explore in unit 12.

But when the lines are spoken aloud in **context** (that is, when you see the whole situation) they become easier to understand. The actor's tone of voice, the volume of their speech and, of course, what they are doing with their face and hands makes the gist of what they are saying clearer.

● Working in pairs, imagine a very windy day. One of you is trying to get a message across to the other who is standing on the other side of a busy road. Take it in turns to choose one of the following messages which you must try to get the other one to understand. The way to do this is to mouth the words as if the wind has, in effect, turned your volume control down so you will have to resort to making other signs to get your meaning across.

You've missed your bus!
Is my homework book in your bag?
Can you come down to the park tonight?
It's very windy today!

● Now make up a message of your own. Talk about what techniques you used to try to show/understand what was being said.

● Now read this section from the opening of Shakespeare's play *The Tempest*.

BOATSWAIN   Down with the topmast! yare! lower, lower! Bring her to try with main-course. [*A cry within.*] A plague upon this howling! They are louder than the weather or our office.

[*Enter* SEBASTIAN, ANTONIO *and* GONZALO.]

Yet again! What do you here? Shall we give o'er, and drown? Have you a mind to sink?   5

SEBASTIAN   A pox o' your throat, you bawling, blasphemous, incharitable dog!

BOATSWAIN   Work you then?

ANTONIO   Hang, cur! hang, you whoreson, insolent noise-maker. We
are less afraid to be drowned than thou art.   10
GONZALO   I'll warrant him for drowning, though the ship were no
stronger than a nutshell, and as leaky as an unstanched wench.
BOATSWAIN   Lay her a-hold, a-hold! set her two courses; off to sea
again; lay her off.

[*Enter* MARINERS, *wet.*]

MARINERS   All lost, to prayers, to prayers! All lost!   15

● What do you think the context is for this scene? What's going on? (Yes, the
play's title is a clue!) As a whole class, use your voices to create a **soundscape**
for this scene, that is, make your own background sound effects. Some members
of the class should try to speak the lines of the scene aloud over the top of your
sound effects.
● What general effect is Shakespeare trying to achieve here?

This next extract comes from *Billy Liar* by Keith Waterhouse and Willis Hall.
● Read it through in pairs and then start to rehearse what you think the best
way would be to use your voices to show what's going on.

GEOFFREY   By bloody hell! I'll give you 'what' if you don't stop saying
'what, what' my lad! You know what. Don't think I haven't been
talking to Mr Duxbury – because I have. I've heard it all. You make
me a laughing-stock. You can't keep your hands off nothing. And
where's that monkey-wrench out of my garage? I suppose you know   5
nothing about that?
BILLY   No, 'course I don't. What do I want with a monkey-wrench?
GEOFFREY   What do you want with two hundred bloody calendars!
And what have you been doing with their name-plates as well?
You're not right in the bloody head.   10
BILLY   I'm not right! I'm not right! I didn't want to work for Shadrack
and flaming Duxbury's! You made me take the rotten job! Now you
can answer for it.
GEOFFREY   Don't bloody shout at me, you gormless young get – or I'll
knock your eyes out.   15
BILLY   God give me strength.
GEOFFREY   Give you strength, he wants to give you some sense! You're

like a bloody Mary-Ann! Well, I hope your mother gets more sense out of you.

● What words and other clues are there here that tell you plainly that these two characters are having an argument?
● Pick out all the words and phrases in this extract which you think readers will find difficult in 400 years' time.
● Do you think readers in 400 years' time will be able to understand anything from this passage? What will help them?

You can't shout all the time!

Variations in volume can have great dramatic effect for an audience. Obviously, if the actors operate at full volume the whole time they will get tired and so will the audience. If everyone on stage whispers all the time, the audience will eventually lose interest and give up. But sudden or gradual changes in spoken volume can keep the audience's attention very effectively.
● In pairs, try this moment from Shakespeare's play *Much Ado About Nothing*. Benedick asks Beatrice what he can do to help her and to prove his love for her, and gets a surprise answer. As you practise the words, try to find two places where you want to make a definite change of volume, either up or down.

BEATRICE   You have stayed me in a happy hour. I was about to protest I loved you.
BENEDICK   And do it with all thy heart.
BEATRICE   I love you with so much of my heart, that none is left to protest.   5
BENEDICK   Come bid me do anything for thee.
BEATRICE   Kill Claudio.
BENEDICK   Ha! not for the wide world.
BEATRICE   You kill me to deny it. Farewell.
BENEDICK   Tarry, sweet Beatrice.   10

[*He holds her.*]

BEATRICE   I am gone, though I am here – there is no love in you – nay, I pray you let me go!
BENEDICK   Beatrice –
BEATRICE   In faith, I will go!

BENEDICK   We'll be friends first.   15

[*He lets her go.*]

BEATRICE   You dare easier be friends with me than fight with mine
enemy?

BENEDICK   Is Claudio thine enemy?

BEATRICE   Is 'a not approved in the height a villain, that hath slan-
dered, scorned, dishonoured my kinswoman? O that I were a man!   20
What, bear her in hand until they come to take hands, and then
with public accusation, uncovered slander, unmitigated rancour – O
God, that I were a man! I would eat his heart in the market place.

BENEDICK   Hear me, Beatrice –

Unit 9   Dialogue

Open most plays at any page and the obvious thing that will strike you as being
different from a novel will be the way the page is set out. Down the left-hand
side you will most likely see the names of various characters, and next to the
names you will read what they are saying, the **dialogue**.

In this unit you will discover that writing plays involves a lot more than simply putting down on paper what people say in real life.

● In pairs, try out this piece of dialogue in at least six different ways:

---

1   Good morning!
2   I beg your pardon?
1   I said, 'Good morning'.
2   I'm not so sure about that.

You may try changing the volume or adding pauses. Perhaps you can experiment
with your tone of voice. If you have enough space, try moving on different lines
or experiment with the different effects of sitting or standing.

● Now decide on a situation in which you think this conversation might take
place. You might decide, for example, that 1 is a groom who has just arrived at
the altar to meet 2, his wife-to-be who has already been waiting for 30 minutes.
Having decided on the context for the dialogue, rehearse it again and try to find
ways of making it clear to the audience who you are and where you are without
adding any more lines.

● Share your work and listen to the audience's comments to see how successful you have been in making the situation clear. Try to pinpoint exactly how you managed this.

● In pairs, write a four-line play of your own. The first thing to do is to think of a situation. You could start by improvising a whole scene, then selecting four lines that capture the essence of the situation and the relationship between the two characters.

● Once you've written down your four lines, pass them to another pair but tell them nothing about the characters or the situation as you imagined it. They must now rehearse the play in their own way.

When these scenes are shared you will have lots to talk about:

How did the performers imagine the scene?

Why did they make their decisions about how to play the scene?

'Dialogue' is the word we use for what characters actually say to each other in a play but, clearly, making a play involves more than just recording speech. If you were to hold a tape recorder up and record a group of people talking you will find, when you play it back, a lot of differences between 'real' speech and 'dramatic' speech. People talk over each other, they don't finish sentences and it's often a complete mystery to the listener what they are actually talking about: talkers often share a knowledge of a subject which the listener does not have, so they don't need to give too many details.

In a play, though, the dialogue must be written so that the audience will be interested in, and can follow, what's going on. It would also be a bit pointless going to the theatre just to hear what we can hear on an average day; we want to see and hear something more interesting happening. We want to see characters develop and a story unfold. The dialogue has to be very carefully chosen if this is to happen yet, at the same time, the audience often needs to be given the impression that what they are hearing and seeing is believable.

Although the dialogue in a play may seem just like everyday speech, playwrights often try to make it clear through what is being said what is actually happening rather than writing a stage direction for every single action:

MEG   Let's have some of yours.

MCCANN   In that?

MEG   Yes.

MCCANN   Are you used to mixing them?

MEG   No.   5

MCCANN   Give me your glass.

from *The Birthday Party* by Harold Pinter

38

● What do you think is actually going on in this scene? What are the actors actually doing? In pairs, act out the scene and put in the appropriate actions.
● Write a short piece of dialogue of your own in which the words spoken make it absolutely clear what action is taking place.

Some writers go further in actually trying to capture the sense of 'realness' in the way they set out the dialogue on the page. Caryl Churchill puts a / in the line to show when the next speaker ought to start even though the first speaker hasn't finished. Sometimes she puts a / at the end of the line to indicate that the speaker is ploughing on regardless of any interruption.

MARGARET   Weirdos and winos, about it with her, all she can get.
   There was one looked like a goldfish couldn't shut his mouth come
   in handy I suppose with the kissing, surprised you can shut yours /
   all the time you spend round
FRANK   You fancy Charlie.   5
MARGARET   there, want to watch out you don't end up looking like a
   goldfish. I do not fancy Charlie /
FRANK   You like him don't you?
MARGARET   so don't start that. I quite like him. He's your friend.
   You're the one he tells /   10
FRANK   We all know whose friend he is, you like him don't you?
MARGARET   lies for. Your friend. I don't like him / like
FRANK   You fancy him.
MARGARET   that, I quite like him.

from *Three More Sleepless Nights* by Caryl Churchill

● In pairs, try to rehearse this dialogue. You may well find it surprisingly difficult to do, even though this is pretty much how people tend to speak naturally to each other in everyday life.
● Improvise a short scene of your own in which A is accusing B of stealing something but B is denying the accusation. Write down at least ten lines of the improvisation, using Caryl Churchill's technique to show where the speakers cut across each other.

Giving the game away

Some plays simply do not convince an audience because the playwright is too anxious to give the audience too much background knowledge of the characters and the situation. In his play *The Real Inspector Hound*, playwright Tom Stoppard mocks the way poorly written thrillers are written. Read here how the house-keeper – unconvincingly named Mrs Drudge – answers the telephone:

Hello, the drawing-room of Lady Muldoon's country residence one morning
in early spring? . . . Hello! – the draw – Who? Who did you wish to speak to?
I'm afraid there is no one of that name here, this is all very mysterious and
I'm sure it's leading up to something, I hope nothing is amiss for we, that is
Lady Muldoon and her houseguests, are here cut off from the world, includ-   5
ing Magnus, the wheelchair-ridden half-brother of her ladyship's husband
Lord Albert Muldoon who ten years ago went out for a walk on the cliffs and
was never seen again – and all alone, for they had no children . . . Should a
stranger enter our midst, which I very much doubt, I will tell him you called.
Goodbye.   10

One way of avoiding telling the audience too much all in one go is to deliber-ately leave gaps in the script so that the audience gets the impression that what
is being said is just the tip of the iceberg of what is actually going on.
● Read the following extract from *Home* by David Storey. Watch out for those
moments when the conversation seems to jump from one thing to another. From
this we might get a number of impressions that make the characters seem believ-able. In pairs, try out this conversation in the following four ways. For example,
try it as if the two men:
   are old acquaintances who meet regularly
   are a little mistrustful of each other
   are just talking for the sake of it and don't actually know each other terribly
   well
   each have something else on their mind that they find difficult to talk about.
● Notice also how the playwright gives us the idea that the two of them are in
a real world of their own and have their own life stories, but the audience can
only glimpse bits of this.

JACK   I say. That was a shock.
HARRY   Yesterday . . .?
JACK   Bolt from the blue, and no mistake.
HARRY   I'd been half-prepared – even then.
JACK   Still: a shock.   5

HARRY   Absolutely.

JACK   My wife – you've met? – was that last week?

HARRY   Ah, yes . . .

JACK   Well. A very delicate woman.

HARRY   Still. Very sturdy.   10

JACK   Oh, well. Physically, nothing to complain of.

HARRY   Oh, no.

JACK   Temperament, however . . . inclined to the sensitive side.

HARRY   Really.

JACK   Two years ago . . . [*He glances off stage.*] By Jove. Isn't that   15
Saxton?

HARRY   Believe it is.

JACK   He's a sharp dresser, and no mistake.

HARRY   Very.

JACK   They tell me . . . Well, I never.   20

HARRY   Didn't see that, did he? [*They laugh, looking off.*] Eyes in the
back of your head these days.

JACK   You have. That's right.

HARRY   Won't do that again in a hurry. What? [*He laughs.*]

JACK   I had an uncle once who bred horses.   25

HARRY   Really.

JACK   Used to go down there when I was a boy.

HARRY   The country.

JACK   Nothing like it. What? Fresh air.

HARRY   Clouds. [*He gestures up.*]   30

JACK   I'd say so.

HARRY   My wife was coming up this morning.

JACK   Really?

HARRY   Slight headache. Thought might be better . . .

JACK   Indoors. Well. Best make sure.   35

At the start of the play *Home* the audience is not at all sure who Harry and Jack
are, where they are and what their relationship is. By the end, though, we realise
that they are patients in a mental hospital who have suffered some kind of
nervous breakdown. We are never told this exactly, but we arrive at the conclusion because of the way David Storey shows us more and more little glimpses
of their lives through what they say and, perhaps more importantly, what they
avoid saying.

● Perhaps the best way to perform the dialogue is by mixing all four of the ways
noted above. Try it.

● Now try out this little experiment in scriptwriting. In pairs, imagine that one of you is a teenager who wants to go out and the other a parent who has a number of reasons for not letting them. Each line spoken must start with a new letter of the alphabet in sequence, for example:

---

1   Andrew, you are not going out tonight and that's final.
2   But Mum . . .
1   Crumbs! Is that the time already?
2   Dad would let me go if he was here.
1   Enough of this. Now let me get on.

● Work in pairs to make up your own version of this conversation. Write it out clearly on a separate sheet. Try to get down the alphabet at least as far as M.
● Pass your script on to another pair and rehearse the one you receive in return. Where are the 'gaps' and jumps in the dialogue? To what extent do you think this made the dialogue feel 'real' even though it was written to this rigid rule?

Playwrights do not, as a rule, tend to use such a bizarre constraint as following the alphabet. A sense of authenticity can be put into dialogue in many ways, for example:
   stopping the line half way through a sentence
   having the characters allude to something that the audience may not know about
   changing the subject suddenly
   going back to something mentioned before.
● Read this made up example, then write a short example of your own:

---

1   So, did you go and see her?
2   Oh yes. Have you . . .?
1   No. No, I haven't had time. That job I told you about.
2   Coming on alright?
1   Yes, fine. Little bit of trouble with the wiring. [*Pause.*] How was she then?
2   Well, it's not looking too good.
1   What you thought?
2   Yeah. I think so.

Unit 10   And now for the news . . .

Plays aren't always just about what people say to each other. Playwrights use all sorts of ways of giving important information to the audience. Look at these snippets from plays:

FIRST NEWSBOY   Special! Austria declares war on Serbia!
SECOND NEWSBOY   Extra! Russia mobilizes! Russia mobilizes!

from *Oh What a Lovely War* by Theatre Workshop

SANDRA   Shut up a minute. They're saying someat.

[*She reaches towards the radio. Momentary blackout. The scene lit, with overhead spot, on the radio. The actors freeze.*]

RECORDING ANNOUNCER   The Prime Minister, The Rt. Hon. Winston Churchill.
CHURCHILL   Yesterday morning at 2.41am at General Eisenhower's headquarters, General Jodl, the representative of the German High   5
Command, and the Grand-Admiral Doenitz, the designated head of the German state, signed the act of unconditional surrender of all German Land, Sea and Air Forces in Europe.

from *Touched* by Stephen Lowe

CAPTAIN   Dictation.
BOY   Yes, Captain.
CAPTAIN   Our last port of call on the African coast. Only three slaves of the last batch of forty have died on the six day river passage. May God be thanked for it. We have branded and documented and all   5
slaves are now insured against death on route to the Indies. They are exercised daily in the hope that fresh air will reduce disease. One cup of maize porridge per slave per day should ensure that stores are sufficient for the voyage.

from *Anansi* by Alistair Campbell

43

• Think about the plays and films that you have seen. Can you remember at least five more methods used to give the audience information about where and when the action is taking place and what is happening?

• Choose one of your ideas above and write a short script which uses the method to tell the audience something important.

Unit 11   Direct address

Direct and aside

• Read the following two short extracts:

CYRIL [*To audience.*]   Ladies and gentlemen, sex as a blood sport: the thrill of the chase; run to earth, there for the kill. Once our affair was established, I surprised myself by continuing to enjoy it . . . thoroughly! Dear Betsy saw a life of perpetual bliss spread out before us like some magical oriental carpet. Whereas I, who had no intention   5 of wedding her, began to consider what danger the poor child stood in should the affair be discovered. She was young and I was excessively fond of her. I had no wish to see her come to grief.

from *Moll Flanders* by Claire Luckham

THE TEACHER   I am the teacher. I keep a school in the city and I have a pupil whose father is dead; he has only his mother to look after him. Now I will go and say good-bye to them, for I shall soon be starting on a journey to the mountains. A terrible disease has broken out among us, and in the city beyond the mountains live sev-   5 eral great doctors.

from *He Who Says Yes* by Bertolt Brecht

• Talk about:
who the characters are actually speaking to here
what the function of their speech seems to be.

When a character in a play 'steps out of the action' and talks to the audience it is called **direct address**. The technique is used for many different purposes, such as:

44

allowing characters to introduce themselves to the audience
giving the audience essential information about what is happening and why
reminding the audience that they are watching a play rather than a piece of
real life.

Sometimes direct address is used to tell the audience what to expect in the
play:

NARRATOR   We are here today to tell you the story of what happened
very recently in a small fishing village in Japan called Minamata.
You'll see in a short while why the people of that village want all the
world to know what has happened to them. We are not from Japan.
But we want to try to tell this story in a Japanese way.   5
from Drink the Mercury by Belgrade TIE Co.

Sometimes direct address is used to make the audience watching the play feel as
if they are in fact watching a different show in a different time and place:

VOICE   And now, ladies and gentlemen, let's hear it for Buffalo Bill's
fantastic company of authentic Western heroes . . . the fabulous
ROUGHRIDERS OF THE WORLD!
With the ever-lovely . . . ANNIE OAKLEY!
And now, once again, here he is – the star of our show, the Ol'   5
Scout himself; I mean the indestructible and ever-popular –
BUFFALO BILL!
from Indians by Arthur Kopit

And sometimes a character lets the audience in on what he or she is thinking:

CYRIL   Trust me. Trust me. I adore you.
MOLL   Trust you? [*Aside.*] If only he knew, I trust him absolutely and
completely. I would walk barefoot to China with him! [*To* CYRIL.]
Oh Cyril, you don't know what you're asking.
from Moll Flanders by Claire Luckham

This last example in which the actor stays in role as the character but talks to us is called an **aside**. A common way of performing an aside is for the actor to turn towards the audience and shield her mouth from the other characters on stage with her hand, as if she is whispering something secret to us.

● In groups, choose a well-known fairy story and re-enact it using different kinds of direct address. Try to use the technique to:

make the story clear

help the audience understand why you are performing it in the way you are introduce the characters

help the audience understand more about what the characters are thinking.

Speak your mind

Playwrights sometimes want the audience to know exactly what a particular character is thinking, but want to keep a distance between the character and the audience. With an aside, the character is deliberately letting the audience in on their thinking. However, there is another technique called **soliloquy** which works by the character speaking his thoughts aloud as if he were entirely on his own. Perhaps the most famous example of a soliloquy is Hamlet's lines when he is considering whether or not to commit suicide:

To be, or not to be. That is the question.
Whether 'tis nobler in the mind to suffer
The slings and arrows of outrageous fortune
Or to take arms against a sea of troubles
And by opposing end them?   5

A soliloquy is a special form of **monologue**. Monologue simply means a speech given by one character who is, generally speaking, alone on the stage – they might be talking to the audience or another character who the audience cannot actually see.

Effective pieces of drama can be made by mixing up what different characters are saying, even though they are not actually talking to each other. In the following extract, from *Oh What a Lovely War* by Theatre Workshop, three separate characters are praying before the start of the Battle of the Somme. It's almost as if three separate soliloquies have been cut together to show the contrast between the way the characters are speaking their minds:

NURSE   The fields are full of tents, O Lord, all empty except for as yet
unmade and naked iron bedsteads. Every ward has been cleared to
make way for the wounded that will be arriving when the big push
comes.

HAIG   I trust you will understand, Lord, that as a British gentleman I   5
could not subordinate myself to the ambitions of a junior foreign
commander, as the politicians suggested. It is for the prestige of my
King and Empire, Lord.

CHAPLAIN   Teach us to rule ourself alway, controlled and cleanly night
and day.   10

HAIG   I ask thee for victory, Lord, before the Americans arrive.

NURSE   The doctors say there will be enormous numbers of dead and
wounded, God.

CHAPLAIN   That we may bring if need arise, no maimed or worthless
sacrifice.   15

HAIG   Thus to grant us fair weather for tomorrow's attack, that we
may drive the enemy into the sea.

NURSE   O Lord, I beg you, do not let this dreadful war cause all the suffering that we have prepared for. I know you will answer my prayer.

[*Explosion. They go off.*]

from *Oh What a Lovely War* by Theatre Workshop

● Talk about the overall effect of this scene. What does it say to you about attitudes towards war and the people involved in it? Do you think cutting the three
prayers together worked dramatically? Can you say why?

● What effect does the final stage direction have on your attitude towards the
characters?

● What do you think each character's attitude to the other two would be if they
could hear each other's prayers? Copy the diagram below and write a line that
they may say to each other under each of the arrows. An example is given:

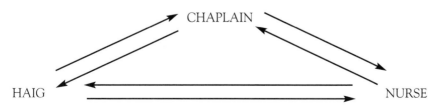

You must understand, dear, that in war some loss of life is absolutely necessary.

47

● Write a monologue for either the Nurse, Haig or the Chaplain which could be spoken after the terrible battle. Remember, in a monologue the character could be talking to us, the audience or another character (or characters) who we cannot see. Here are some examples to help you:

The Chaplain talks to the audience as if they are a congregation of soldiers.

The Nurse tells the audience directly how she felt when the wounded started to arrive.

General Haig makes a speech defending his decision to press ahead with the battle plan.

● Experiment with this idea of cutting monologues/soliloquies together. Work in pairs. Write a scene in which two characters are somehow involved in the same situation and are speaking aloud (but not actually to each other) by using one of the ideas in column A below and one in column B.

Keep the scene going by alternating back and forth between the two characters. Agree on a title for the scene which would fit both situations.

A	B
A child is writing to Santa saying what they want for Christmas.	A news reporter is giving the first details of an air crash.
A doctor is filling in a report on a patient who is seriously ill.	Someone is speaking to a friend on telephone about their forthcoming holiday.
A customer in a restaurant ordering a meal.	A teacher in a staffroom complaining about a particular student.
A teenager is writing a love letter to someone they have been after for months but have been too shy to talk to directly.	A character is writing their personal thoughts in their diary about the events of the previous week.

Unit 12   Rhythm

Have you ever had the unfortunate experience of being talked to by someone whose voice just seems to drone on and on? Playwrights are very aware that if they don't write a character's lines with some sense of rhythm there is only so much actors can do to make the lines sound interesting on stage.

Sometimes playwrights use very special rhythms to make the lines sound almost like songs. The words become good to listen to and set up a particular atmosphere.

● Stand in a circle and read aloud just one line each of this opening section of
Lin Coghlan's play A *Feeling in My Bones*:

VOICE Night time coming
The snow falling gently
The shadows growing longer
The house silent, empty
Like a shell.   5
Beep! Beep!
MUM Sean! Come on love!
SEAN Alright.
VOICE The wind is blowing from the south
Up over the dark top of West Hill   10
And across the backs of the brown and white
Cows in the little paddock
And over the branches of the fallen tree
Down by the Lower Road
Rattling now on the front door.   15
The boy puts his ear to the
Empty shell of a house
And hears the beginning
All over again.
MUM Is there a sleeping person in there?   20
SEAN Yes, I'm asleep.
VOICE Buried underneath the patchwork blanket Granny made
Wild birds crying in the bare trees.
MUM Sean! It's snowing!
VOICE White white   25
Right up over the West Hill
With the crows circling the frosted fields
And powder resting on the fence
Down by the little paddock.

● Now read the lines aloud again:
    as if you are out of breath
    as if you are a vicar speaking at a funeral
    as if you are a bus conductor announcing the next stop
    as if you are the sexiest person in the world.

• Read your own line again and again until you know it off by heart. Play around with different ways of saying it. Listen to the sounds of the words and fix on what you think is the 'right' way of speaking it.

• Stand in a circle again and, with your eyes closed, speak the lines aloud in order in the way you have decided. Listen carefully to each other as you do this.

• What words or phrases would you use to describe the atmosphere being created by these lines?

• It is quite difficult to work out exactly what is happening in this play opening. Things don't seem to be happening in any clear order. One way of finding out what is important in the lines is to go through them on your own and pick out any words that you think sound particularly good or are repeated.

• When you have done this, stand in a circle again. This time have just one person reading the whole passage. Every time the reader reaches a word you have underlined, quietly echo that word.

• Talk about which words seem to be echoed the most. Why do you think that is?

• Look back at the passage again and make a copy of it. To the left of the lines on your copy, draw arrows to show where there seem to be jumps and breaks in the rhythm. To the right of the lines, draw wavy lines to show where the rhythm seems to flow.

• Talk about the effect of having some lines flowing and others seeming to jump. Why do you think the writer used this technique? What might this suggest about the place where Sean and his Mum live and the different things happening there?

On stage, the action of the play needs to reflect the rhythm of the lines and vice versa. In *Romeo and Juliet*, Romeo goes to a ball being held at Juliet's house. It is here that he first spots Juliet and the two are immediately attracted to each other. Try this exercise to explore how Shakespeare uses the situation of the party to bring together the two young lovers:

• Find a partner and number yourselves A and B, then stand next to each other in a large circle. As should turn to face right and Bs should turn to face left so that each 'couple' are now facing each other. Put your hands up to the level of your shoulders as if you are surrendering to someone.

• As should now walk around the circle anti-clockwise, very slowly weaving in and out of the Bs who will stand still. As the As pass around, they should very lightly put the palm of their hand against the palm of B's hand, first right hand to right hand and then, with the next B they pass, left hand to left hand.

• Once you've got the idea of this, the Bs could start to move slowly around the circle in a clockwise direction. Again, the idea is to put palm to palm as you pass each other.

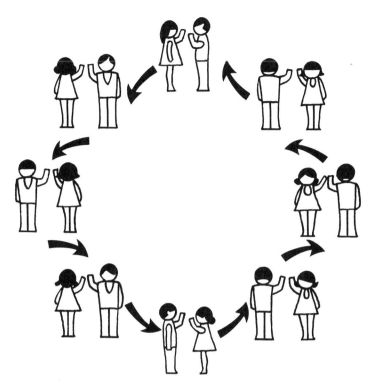

The Elizabethans would have used a similar sort of pattern to dance a rather stately dance called a galliard. You could try moving around the circle like this in time to a piece of Elizabethan galliard music.

● Now read what happens when Romeo and Juliet actually meet. While two people read these lines slowly aloud, another two could face each other and just keep putting the palms of their hands together as in the circle dance described above. How does the rhythm of the words reflect this action?

ROMEO   If I profane with my unworthiest hand
        This holy shrine, the gentle sin is this:
        My lips, two blushing pilgrims, ready stand
        To smooth that rough touch with a tender kiss.
JULIET   Good pilgrim, you do wrong your hand too much,   5
        Which mannerly devotion shows in this;
        For saints have hands that pilgrims' hands do touch,
        And palm to palm is holy palmers' kiss.
ROMEO   Have not saints lips, and holy palmers too?

JULIET   Ay, pilgrim, lips that they must use in prayer.   10
ROMEO   O then, dear saint, let lips do what hands do!
              They pray 'Grant thou, lest faith turn to despair.'
JULIET   Saints do not move, though grant for prayer's sake.
ROMEO   Then move not, while my prayer's effect I take.

[*He kisses her.*]

Apart from when they were dancing, the Elizabethans would certainly have put their own palms together when they were praying. A 'palmer' was a person who had been on a pilgrimage to the Holy Land and carried a palm leaf to show that.
● Pick out all the words in the extract which suggest prayer and holiness. Then list any words which suggest that Romeo and Juliet are worshipping each other in their minds.

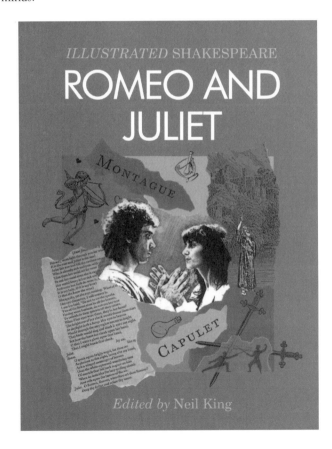

Unit 13   Rhythm in conversation

Everyday conversations have their own rhythm which reflects the mood of the speakers.

● Read this extract from Harold Pinter's play *The Birthday Party* out loud with a partner:

MEG   I've got your cornflakes ready [*She disappears and re-appears.*]
Here's your cornflakes.

[*He rises and takes the plate from her, sits at the table, props up the paper and begins to eat.* MEG *enters by the kitchen door.*]

Are they nice?
PETEY   Very nice.
MEG   I thought they'd be nice. [*She sits at the table.*] You got your   5
paper?
PETEY   Yes.
MEG   Is it good?
PETEY   Not bad.
MEG   What does it say?   10
PETEY   Nothing much.
MEG   You read me out some nice bits yesterday.
PETEY   Yes, well, I haven't finished this one yet.
MEG   Will you tell me when you come to something good?
PETEY   Yes.   15

● How would you describe the mood of this conversation?
● What does it tell you about the sort of characters Meg and Petey are and the kind of life they lead?
● Now look at the way the theatre company Forkbeard Fantasy have written these lines for some characters in their play *Work Ethic*:

TERRY   Hello Suzie. Hello Benny!
MS PRIM   Hello Terry.
SKINNER   Hello Terry . . . how's the Audi?
TERRY   Sold the Audi, got a Volvo. Here comes Simon.

[*Enter* SIMON.]

53

SIMON   Nice one Terry!   5
TERRY   Hello Simon!
SIMON   Hello Suzie!
    Hello Benny. How's our Egg-head?
TERRY   Brainsy Benny . . . Where's the Peugeot?
BENNY   Sold the Peugeot, got an Audi.   10

[*Enter* TRACEY.]

TRACEY   Wotcha Benny. Hello Terry! Hello Suzie!
BENNY   Wotcha Tracey!
TERRY   Hello darlin'!
TRACEY   Watch it, Terry.
MS PRIM   Hello Tracey, love those earrings.   15
TRACEY   Got them Thursday. Texas Homecare.
BENNY   Like the hairdo. How's the Polo?
TRACEY   Sold the Polo, got a Peugeot.
SIMON   Here comes Danny! Hallo Danny, love the shell-suit!

[*Enter* DANNY.]

DANNY   Marks and Spencers. Hello Benny.   20
BENNY   Hello Danny.
TERRY   Wotcha Dan Boy!
DANNY   Simon! Terry! Nice one Tracey! Dig those earrings.
TRACEY   Thank you Danny! Love those trainers.
DANNY   Nice one Tracey . . . what a hairdo!   25
TRACEY   Thank you Danny. Hello Andy! Like the earring!

[*Enter* ANDY.]

ANDY   Hello Tracey, bought it Sunday, down the Car Boot. Hello
    Benny. Hello Suzie.
SUZIE   Hello Simon.
TERRY   Hello Andy!   30
ANDY   Terry! Nice one! Hello Debbie!

[*Enter* DEBBIE.]

● In pairs, read these lines aloud at different speeds. What speed do you think
they want to seem to go at?
● Where do you think the characters are when they speak these lines? What
impression do they seem to want to give each other? How do you know?
● Working on your own or in pairs, write two short conversations. One should

give the impression that the characters are rather bored and perhaps boring, the other should show that the characters are full of life and quite excitable. To do this you will need to think about what the characters are actually talking about and how they respond to each other. Look back at the extract from *The Birthday Party* and you will see that Petey always gives Meg negative answers as if he just wants her to shut up, whereas the characters in *Work Ethic* respond positively to each other (even though they're hardly saying anything important!).

A stick of what?

No, not a stick of anything but **stichomythia**. That's the word that's used for the technique of giving characters a sequence of very short lines which bounce off each other as if the characters are playing a sort of verbal tennis. We've all had the experience of thinking up really clever put downs that we might have used in an argument – the trouble is, by the time we've thought of them the moment to use them has been lost! Playwrights have the benefit of being able to think out their characters' dialogue very carefully beforehand which can make the play very amusing, if not quite believable.

A fine example of stichomythia occurs in Noel Greig's play *Final Cargo*:

ENGINEER   The only question we'll ask is the size of the pay-packet.
SKIPPER   Fair question. Fair size.
ENGINEER   Fair answer.

In this example the same word – 'fair' – is picked up and bounced back. In the following scene from Shakespeare's *The Taming of the Shrew* Petruchio is trying to woo the fiery Kate. Note how in this example it is the idea that is being bounced back and forth as the two characters try to score points off each other.

KATHERINA   If you strike me, you are no gentleman,
   And if no gentleman, why then no arms.
PETRUCHIO   A herald, Kate? O, put me in thy books!
KATHERINA   What is your crest – a coxcomb?
PETRUCHIO   A combless cock, so Kate will be my hen.   5
KATHERINA   No cock of mine, you crow too like a craven.
PETRUCHIO   Nay, come, Kate, come, you must look not sour.

KATHERINA   It is my fashion when I see a crab.
PETRUCHIO   Why, here's no crab, and therefore look not sour.
KATHERINA   There is, there is.   10
PETRUCHIO   Then show it me.
KATHERINA   Had I a glass, I would.
PETRUCHIO   What, you mean my face?
KATHERINA   Well aimed of such a young one.
PETRUCHIO   Now, by Saint George, I am too young for you.   15
KATHERINA   Yet you are withered.
PETRUCHIO   'Tis with cares.
KATHERINA   I care not.

● In pairs, rehearse this dialogue, trying to get the pace as fast as you can without mumbling or spluttering the words.

● Just for an exercise, have a quick game of 'knee boxing' – face each other and try to tap your opponent on the knee. While you are doing this try to convince your opponent that you are much better at the game than they are.

● Now try to add some movements to the dialogue above, using the same sort of physical energy you needed to speak while knee boxing.

● What words and phrases in the dialogue suggest a particular movement or gesture which the characters might use to show exactly what they mean? Rehearse the scene again using these gestures.

Playwright Harold Pinter uses the same technique but to a very different effect in his play *The Birthday Party*. In the scene below stichomythia is used to create a very threatening atmosphere.

● As a warm up to the next exercise, sit facing a partner and simply try to out-stare each other.

● Now take it in turns to say 'Banana' to each other. You can say the word however you like – the more ways the better in fact! The first one of you to smile or laugh is the loser!

In the extract below, two men, Goldberg and McCann are 'interrogating' Stanley. Read through this extract and then, in threes, carry on the interrogation using your own words.

GOLDBERG   When did you come to this place?
STANLEY   Last year.
GOLDBERG   Where did you come from?
STANLEY   Somewhere else.

GOLDBERG Why did you come here?   5
STANLEY My feet hurt!
GOLDBERG Why did you stay?
STANLEY I had a headache.
GOLDBERG Did you take anything for it?
STANLEY Yes.   10
GOLDBERG What?
STANLEY Fruit salts!
GOLDBERG Enos or Andrews?
STANLEY En – An –
GOLDBERG Did you stir properly? Did they fizz?   15
STANLEY Now, now, wait, you –
GOLDBERG Did they fizz? Did they fizz or didn't they fizz?
MCCANN He doesn't know!

● Try out the dialogue and your own improvisation again in the following ways:
   Stanley is seated, Goldberg and McCann are standing over him.
   Stanley is seated, Goldberg and McCann are moving around him.
   All three are moving around.
● Talk about which method worked best in creating a sense of threat.

Unit 14 What's my line?

● Look at the pictures of characters from some famous plays on page 58. Take a careful note of the costumes and make-up they are wearing.
● Beneath the pictures are the characters' names and examples of lines they say in the play. Can you match the names with the pictures and suggest which lines should go with each character?

Mother Courage   Buffalo Bill   Richard III

Lord Foppington   Sir William Harcourt Courtly

1 Well, 'tis an unspeakable pleasure to be a man of quality . . . let my people dispose the glasses so that I may see myself before and behind, for I love to see myself all raund.

2 They're so hungry I've seen 'em digging up roots to eat. I could boil your leather belt and make their mouths water.

3 I have seen sunrise frequently after a ball or from the window of my travelling carriage, and I always considered it disagreeable.

4 I am determined to prove a villain
And hate the idle pleasures of these days.
Plots have I laid . . .

5 Well I'd knocked off 'bout thirty o' their number when I realised I was out o' bullets. Just at that moment, a arrow whizzed past my head.

● Write another line for each of the characters which you think they might say. Briefly explain why you think your line would fit the character.

Unit 15   First impressions

When you see a play being performed on stage, or watch a film or television drama, there are a number of things which help you build up an understanding of what the drama is going to be like and what sort of characters are going to be in it before it has even started. The title of the drama and the way it is presented on posters and book covers might give you some clues.
● Look at this cover of Chris Bond's play *The Blood of Dracula*. How does the title relate to the images on the cover? Look carefully. Are there any surprises in the image? What might this tell you about the play? Make your own notes about what you see in this picture and what clues they give you about the play.

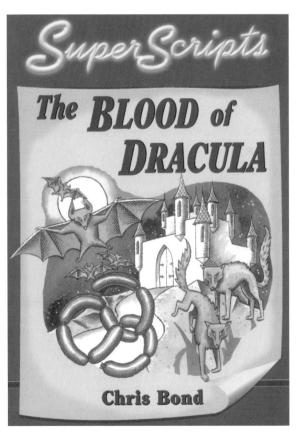

59

● What sort of images would you put on the front cover of these plays that would tell an audience a bit more about the play?

Fifteen Years of a Drunkard's Life
The Alchemist
The Beggar's Opera
The School for Scandal
Lady Audley's Secret

● Devise some titles of your own which you think would leave an audience in little doubt as to the type of play they were about to watch.

● Design an image that could be used as a cover for the script or for a programme that would capture what the play is about.

Unit 16   Moody moments

Once an audience is in the theatre and the action starts, there are many more things that tell them about the type of play they are watching. You can often tell how this will work by looking closely at the language used in the scripts themselves.

● Read the three extracts below. They come from three very different types of play. In each extract somebody is being threatened:

One of the plays is making a serious comment about cruelty and threat.

Another is a **melodrama** which was written in order to excite the audience.

Another sets out to make the audience laugh.

Which one is which?

A

RUTHVEN   I'll hear no more! – she is my bride betrothed: this mad-man would deprive me of her.

RONALD   [*Loud thunder: another gust of wind blows open the casement.*] See! See! The moon already rests upon the wave! – One moment! – but one moment! –   5

RUTHVEN   Nay, then thus I seal my lips, and seize my bride.

[RUTHVEN *draws his poignard: rushes on* RONALD – ROBERT *throws him-self between* RUTHVEN *and* RONALD, *and wrenches the dagger from his grasp.*]

LADY MARGARET   Hold! hold! – I am thine; the moon has set.

RUTHVEN   And I am lost!

[*A terrific peal of thunder is heard;* UNDA *and* ARIEL *appear; a thunder-*

bolt strikes RUTHVEN *to the ground, who immediately vanishes. General picture.*]

The curtain falls.

***

B

[*Music. Thunder.* DRACULA *appears on the stairs blocking their exit.*]

DRACULA   Too late, Doctor. But I believe I have an appointment to view that brooch on your throat.
VAN HELSING   Keep off!

[*She raises crucifix in front of him. He snarls and hisses.*]

HARKER   No, Johnny wants it, keep Johnny safe, Johnny have it!

[*Grabs crucifix. He and* VAN HELSING *struggle over it. It breaks in two pieces.* DRACULA *laughs.*]

HARKER   You broke Johnny's crucifix . . .   5
DRACULA   Now, Doctor . . .
VAN HELSING   The garlic, Sir Robert!

[SEWARD *pulls on* MRS CREBBS' *necklace of garlic. She moans and holds onto it. The string breaks and it rolls all over the floor.*]

SEWARD   It's brock! She's brock the bloody thing!
DRACULA   You see, Doctor, it is useless. Come!
VAN HELSING   No . . .   10
DRACULA   Come!
VAN HELSING   No . . . Please . . .

[*But she moves towards him against her will.*]

SEWARD   What art th' doing, Doctor?
DRACULA   Come!
VAN HELSING   I can't help it . . .   15

[*She is close to* DRACULA *now.*]

DRACULA   Now, Doctor . . . [*Exhales.*] Your brooch . . .

[VAN HELSING *takes choker off.* DRACULA *caresses her neck. He howls like a wolf and is just about to sink his fangs into her when there is music, and a shaft of sunlight lights his face. He screams and leaps into the audience, snarling and fanging them until he reaches the back row.*]

***

C

OFFICER [*To* MAX.]   Who is this man?
MAX   I don't know.

[MAX *stops mumbling. He looks straight ahead.*]

OFFICER   Your friend?

[*Silence.*]

MAX   No.

[RUDY *moans.*]

OFFICER   Look at him. [MAX *stares straight ahead.*] Look! [MAX *looks at*   5
RUDY. *The* OFFICER *hits* RUDY *on the chest.* RUDY *screams.*]
Your friend?
MAX   No.

[*Silence.*]

OFFICER   Hit him.

[MAX *stares at the* OFFICER.]

Like this.   10

[*The* OFFICER *hits* RUDY *on the chest.* RUDY *screams.*]

Hit him.

[MAX *doesn't move.*]

Your friend?

[MAX *doesn't move.*]

Your friend?
MAX   No.

[MAX *closes his eyes. He hits* RUDY *on the chest.* RUDY *screams.*]

OFFICER   Open your eyes.   15

[MAX *opens his eyes.*]

Again.

[MAX *hits* RUDY *in the chest.*]

Again.

[MAX *hits* RUDY *in the chest again and again and again . . .*]

Enough.

[*The* OFFICER *pushes* RUDY *down to the ground, at* MAX's *feet.*]

Your friend?

MAX   No.   20

[*The* OFFICER *smiles.*]

OFFICER   No.

● Under the headings Melodrama, Comedy and Serious, list any lines the characters say which you would use to show that extract **A** is a melodrama, **B** is a comedy and **C** is a play with a serious message.
● Now, under the same headings, list any of the actions that happen on stage which show which extract is which.
● Do you think that any of the situations shown in the extracts are realistic? Can you imagine them actually happening in real life? Does it matter if any of the extracts aren't actually very believable – perhaps they make 'good drama' anyway? Talk about your own ideas on this.

The extracts are from:

A   *The Vampire* by J.R. Planche
B   *The Blood of Dracula* by Chris Bond
C   *Bent* by Martin Sherman.

Unit 17   Genre

Genre is a word that can be used to describe the type of drama you are watching or reading.
● The chart on page 64 lists some examples of different genres that you will have seen on television or on film. Copy out the list of genres and add your own examples. Sometimes, plays and films seem to fit into more than one category. The popular TV series *Red Dwarf*, for example, is science fiction, but it is also a comedy and perhaps even a **satire** (that means it deliberately 'takes the mickey' out of something or someone).

Genres	Examples
Tragedy	*Hamlet, Oedipus the King*
Romance	*Romeo and Juliet*
Situation comedy	*Friends*
Satire	*South Park*
Historical drama	*Schindler's List*
Costume drama	*Pride and Prejudice*
Science fiction	
Farce	
Musical	
Soap opera	
Action/Adventure	

● Look at these cuttings from a copy of the *Radio Times*. From what you know of any of these programmes, and from the descriptions of them printed here, talk about what different genres they seem to be.

9.30   Flowers of the Forest

Choice

A *Screen Two* drama starring **Lia Williams, Pauline Collins, Annette Crosbie.** Two young children are brought to Janet Hinton, a social worker in the Scottish Highlands. When both she and an independent expert become convinced that the children are part of a ritual child abuse network, the small community is thrown into disarray. **See today's choices.**

9.00   Cracker

Choice

A special two-hour episode of the acclaimed police thriller, starring **Robbie Coltrane,** *White Ghost.* While on a lecture tour of Hong Kong, psychologist Fitz is called in to investigate the bizarre murder of a high-flying businessman. Continued after *News at Ten.* **See today's choices.**

6.00   Star Trek: Deep Space Nine

The Search (part 1). Hoping to avert an invasion by the ruthless Jem'Hadar, Sisko takes an experimental warship into the Gamma Quadrant. The story concludes next week.

7.30   Eastenders

Alan presses Frankie for an answer. Lorraine is finding it difficult to cope with David's shortcomings as a parent. Joe makes a dramatic announcement, and Grant attempts a show-down with David.

8.00   Birds of a Feather

Belongings. Sharon is fed up with cooking fried food and decides to give the café a new profile. On Dorien's advice, she opens a bagel bar, but it doesn't go down too well with the local Greek community or husband Chris. Only divine intervention might be able to save the situation.

Looking closely at the language of a piece of drama will help you identify the genre.
● Read through the following three extracts out loud and talk about:
    any 'special' words the characters use that gives clues as to who they are, what they are like and what they think of each other;
    the length of the sentences and punctuation.
● When you have read them through at least three times, talk about what genre you think they might fall into.

A

GILBERT   We're out! We've really made it, Crosby! Oh, *great!* Now we are free! [CROSBY *examines himself, gingerly.*]

GILBERT   Are you all right?

CROSBY   I think you've trodden on my ear. Does it look as if it's swelling up to you?

5

GILBERT   I can't see anything. Never mind your ear – we're out in the open air at last, man! After all that time behind those iron bars – we're free – and it's Christmas Eve – isn't it a terrific feeling?

CROSBY   I'm not sure. I think I felt a speck of rain.

GILBERT   So? Never mind a speck of rain – a drop of water never hurt   10
nobody.

CROSBY   I hate rain, Gilbert. I do, I really hate it. Whenever I'm out in the rain, I seem to get wetter than other people. I think the rain has got it in for me.

B

FREDDIE   I'm sorry, Hes. Oh God, I'm sorry. Please don't cry. You don't know what it does to me.

HESTER   Not now. Not this minute. Not this minute, Freddie?

[FREDDIE *finishes putting on his shoes, and then turns away from her, brushing his sleeve across his eyes.*]

HESTER [*Going to him.*] You've got all your things here. You've got to pack –   5

FREDDIE   I'll send for them.

HESTER   You promised to come back for dinner.

FREDDIE   I know. I'm sorry about that. [*He kisses her quickly and goes to the door.*]

HESTER [*Frantically.*]   But you can't break a promise like that, Freddie.   10
You can't. Come back just for our dinner, Freddie. I won't argue, I swear, and then if you want to go away afterwards –

[FREDDIE *goes out.* HESTER *runs to the door after him.*]

Freddie, come back . . . Don't go . . . Don't leave me alone tonight . . . Not tonight . . . Don't leave me alone tonight . . .

C

STANHOPE   The guns are making a bit of a row.

RALEIGH   Our guns?

STANHOPE   No. Mostly theirs. [*Again there is silence in the dug-out. A very faint rose light is beginning to glow in the dawn sky.* RALEIGH *speaks again – uneasily.*]   5

RALEIGH   I say – Dennis –

STANHOPE   Yes, old boy?

RALEIGH   It – it hasn't gone through, has it? It only just hit me? – and knocked me down?

STANHOPE   It's just gone through a bit, Jimmy.   10

RALEIGH   I won't have to – go on lying here?

STANHOPE   I'm going to have you taken away.

RALEIGH   Away? Where?

STANHOPE   Down to the dressing-station – then hospital – then home.

- Write or improvise the six lines that you think might have come immediately before any one of these extracts. Try to copy, as closely as you can, the style of language and the way the punctuation is used to guide the actors.
- Read or present your lines, along with the original extract, to the rest of the class. Do they agree that you have picked up on the right sort of style?

The extracts are from:

A   *Kidnapped at Christmas* by Willis Hall

B   *The Deep Blue Sea* by Terence Rattigan

C   *Journey's End* by R.C. Sheriff.

Unit 18   Style

It's important to note that **style** and genre are two rather different terms. When we speak of genre we mean the sort of family into which the drama might fall. Style, though, is something more individual to a particular author. For example, the French playwright Georges Feydeau wrote a great many **farces**, as does the English playwright Ray Cooney, but their style is very different.

You might find an illustration of different styles of language in your own classroom:

- In groups of four, each of you should prepare either a short talk about a personal interest or perhaps a story about something that has happened to you.
- Take it in turns to listen to each other speak.
- Are there any words or phrases that the speaker tends to use a lot, for example, 'OK?' or 'Know what I mean?' Do they tend to speak quickly or slowly? How often do they pause? Talk about the different styles of each of the speakers in your group.

Of course, playwrights are in the business of creating fictitious characters and give each of those characters their own style of speech in order to make them interesting and believable. Nevertheless, an experienced reader of plays will recognise that the playwright also has a particular style.

● Look closely at the three extracts below. All three show people in the process of waiting for someone. Two of the extracts are from the same playwright – which two?

A

GUS   What time is he getting in touch?

[BEN *reads.*]

What time is he getting in touch?
BEN   What's the matter with you? It could be any time. Any time.
GUS   [*Moves to the foot of* BEN's *bed.*]   Well, I was going to ask you
     something.   5
BEN   What?
GUS   Have you noticed the time that tank takes to fill?
BEN   What tank?
GUS   In the lavatory.
BEN   No. Does it?   10
GUS   Terrible.
BEN   Well, what about it?
GUS   What do you think's the matter with it?
BEN   Nothing.
GUS   Nothing?   15
BEN   It's got a deficient ballcock, that's all.
GUS   A deficient what?
BEN   Ballcock.
GUS   No? Really?
BEN   That's what I should say.   20
GUS   Go on! That didn't occur to me.

B

ESTRAGON   Charming spot. [*He turns, advances to front, halts facing
    auditorium.*] Inspiring prospects. [*He turns to* VLADIMIR.] Let's go.
VLADIMIR   We can't.
ESTRAGON   Why not?
VLADIMIR   We're waiting for Godot.   5
ESTRAGON   [*Despairingly.*] Ah! [*Pause.*] You're sure it was here?

VLADIMIR What?
ESTRAGON That we were to wait.
VLADIMIR He said by the tree. [*They look at the tree.*] Do you see any
  others?   10
ESTRAGON What is it?
VLADIMIR I don't know. A willow.
ESTRAGON Where are the leaves?
VLADIMIR It must be dead.
ESTRAGON No more weeping.   15
VLADIMIR Or perhaps it's not the season.
ESTRAGON Looks to me more like a bush.
VLADIMIR A shrub.
ESTRAGON A bush.
VLADIMIR A – . What are you insinuating? That we've come to the   20
  wrong place?

C

ROSE What were you looking for?
MRS SANDS The man who runs the house.
MR SANDS The landlord. We're trying to get hold of the landlord.
MRS SANDS What's his name, Toddy?
ROSE His name's Mr Kidd.   5
MRS SANDS Kidd. Was that the name, Toddy?
MR SANDS Kidd? No, that's not it.
ROSE Mr Kidd. That's his name.
MR SANDS Well, that's not the bloke we're looking for.
ROSE Well, you must be looking for someone else.   10

[*Pause.*]

MR SANDS I suppose we must be.
ROSE You look cold.
MRS SANDS It's murder out. Have you been out?
ROSE No.
MRS SANDS We've not long come in.   15
ROSE Well, come inside, if you like, and have a warm.

[*They come into the centre of the room.*]

[*Bringing the chair from the table to the fire.*]

Sit down here. You can get a good warm.

MRS SANDS   Thanks. [*She sits.*]
ROSE   Come over by the fire, Mr Sands.
MR SANDS   No, it's all right. I'll just stretch my legs.   20
MRS SANDS   Why? You haven't been sitting down.
MR SANDS   What about it?
MRS SANDS   Well, why don't you sit down?
MR SANDS   Why should I?
MRS SANDS   You must be cold.   25
MR SANDS   I'm not.

● In pairs, or groups of three, read these extracts aloud. Discuss the 'feel' of each one.

● In all three extracts the characters seem to contradict each other, but do all of the extracts have the same kind of tension?

● In all three extracts, the characters tend to speak in quite short lines, but is there a difference in the way they use language?

● So, which two extracts are by the same playwright? Write a brief explanation of why you think this.

Unit 19   Positioning the audience

Many plays that you read and see attempt to give the audience the illusion that the characters are real. The playwright invites us to watch their lives unfold as if we were a peeping-tom: the characters are unaware of our presence and so say and do things that they'd never say or do if there was a stranger watching (let alone several hundred!).

This type of theatre is often called **naturalistic** because the playwright wants us to believe that the characters are going about their lives as they would naturally. You will certainly be familiar with this type of drama if you watch soap operas such as *EastEnders* or *Neighbours* (in which case several million people are watching the characters say and do some very private things!). So, the playwright is really cheating – what we are being shown isn't natural at all! It isn't just that the rooms in which the characters appear to live are impossible, but what we, the audience, are actually shown of their lives is highly selective; everything we see and hear matters – the playwright is showing us things that will help us make up our minds about the characters. On television and in films the way the camera is used goes even further by making decisions for us regarding exactly who or what we should be looking at at any given moment.

In this way we can say that the audience is being **positioned**. That is, we are being told, to a certain extent, what to think and feel about what is going on.

● In pairs or small groups, talk about a recent episode of a soap opera or drama that you have seen and pick out at least four things that happened which you could believe in as 'natural', that is, they might happen in real life.

● Thinking of the same episode or drama, talk about how you, as a member of the audience, were made to either feel sorry for or dislike for one of the characters.

● Now think of four things from the same drama that would show that it was-n't 'real life' at all.

Not all dramas attempt to make the audience believe that what is going on on stage is real life even if they are telling stories that are true. In fact, looking at plays throughout history, this attempt seems quite a recent invention.

The play *Example*, which was written by the Belgrade Theatre in Education Company, tells the story of Derek Bentley who was hanged for the part he played in the shooting of a policeman in 1953. The case was very controversial – many people thought it was wrong that Bentley was hanged and that he was a victim of the need at the time to make an example of someone in order to try and stamp out crime among young people.

● Read this opening from the play:

[*Introductory music. The newscaster's voice is on tape while the slides are shown on the screen.*]

NEWS   Ladies and gentlemen, the Organisation proudly presents for you Potted Pictorial News Magazine. Once again we bring you the brightest and best in educational news entertainment right into the warmth and comfort of your own school hall. Today we cover the post-war years.   5

[*Loud patriotic music. Slide of VE Day.*]

It's the 15th August 1945, and the whole of a victorious and happy nation is out in the streets to celebrate the ending of World War Two.

Example is a play based on a true story, but how is the audience being 'positioned' here? Where are we being told we are? Who are we being told we are?

● Now look at this speech which comes after the introductory slide show and lecture:

TEACHER   Last night, before you went home, you were all supposed to hand in an essay under the title of 'Where I Live'. From the work I've seen so far, I can only presume that most of you walk the streets at night. One essay – that's all I got. Johnson's. Let me read it to you. 'Where I Live' by P. Johnson, 4B. 'I live at 67, Nuttall Road, 5 Croydon.' Apart from three blots and a crossing out, that's it. And by the way, Johnson, there's no 'u' in road. I don't have to tell you, it's not good enough. Now I don't expect you all to be little Willy Shakespeares. I know that due to the war, most of you haven't had more than one year of school in the last five. But I do expect you to 10 try. This is your last year and my God, I'm going to give you lot some sort of chance even if I have to put half of you in hospital to do it. Oh, and talking of hospitals, I see that we have a little stranger with us this morning. Bentley has decided to honour us with his yearly visit. Come out here, lad! Let's have a look at you. We don't get the 15 chance very often.

[BENTLEY *comes forward.*]

• Read this speech aloud to yourself, imagining that you are addressing a class (perhaps a couple of volunteers could actually address your class while reading these lines).

• Describe how you think the audience would feel having an actor talking to them like this.

• Describe how you think the audience would feel when Bentley is called forward. Say why you think this.

In this scene the audience are being 'positioned' as members of Bentley's own class. The experience of being talked to like this by teachers is, sadly, probably something we have all experienced. You might, as a member of the audience, be tempted to giggle a bit but at the same time be trying not to. Just as in a real classroom, you wouldn't want to draw attention to yourself in such a situation, so in the theatre you might be frightened that the actor playing the teacher will turn on you! Perhaps you would feel a bit relieved when the teacher calls out Bentley, while at the same time feeling a bit sorry for him.

• Now look at how the audience is re-positioned in the next scene:

VOICE OVER (*Tape.*)   Mrs Lilian Bentley. Derek Bentley's mother.

[*Slide of* MRS BENTLEY. *She enters very shaken and upset.* DEREK BENT-LEY *enters. Blank slide.*]

BENTLEY   Hello, Mum.

[MRS BENTLEY *humphs and turns away.*]

What's the matter?
MRS BENTLEY   Don't you know, Derek? Don't you know?
BENTLEY   You're upset, Mum. That's all I know.   5
MRS BENTLEY   Upset? Yes, I am upset! So would you be if you'd had
the police trampling through your house, going through your things,
and not knowing what they wanted.

Here we are being re-positioned and invited to be peeping-toms in Bentley's
house. The scene is naturalistic but we are taking with us into this scene an
impression of Bentley gained from the scene before (where the teacher made a
point of telling Bentley how stupid and pathetic he was). In this way, the audience is being encouraged to see Bentley as somebody who is picked on, an innocent who, as it turns out, was all too easy to make an 'example' of.

Every new thing we see and hear in a play is coloured by what we have seen
and heard already. Re-positioning an audience like this can make us question the
way we look at things and the way we make assumptions about what they mean.
● In groups, devise a short improvisation in which the audience is invited to
either feel very sorry for one of the characters or, alternatively, to see the character as a villain.
● Make a note of some ideas about how the audience might be re-positioned in
order for them to see the character from a different perspective.
● Where do you think these lines originally came from?

Youth, youth, thou hadst better been starved by thy nurse,
Than live to be hanged for cutting a purse.

The lines come from a song that was popular 400 years ago. It warns potential
criminals about how severe punishments were for crimes such as picking pockets.
● Now read the extract below.

COKES   Look you sister, here, here, where is it now? Which pocket is't

73

in, for a wager?

[*He shows his purse again.*]

Sister, I am an ass, I cannot keep my purse?

[*He shows his purse again.*]

On, on, I pray thee, friend.

NIGHTINGALE [*Sings.*]   Repent then, repent you, for better, for worse,   5
And kiss not the gallows for cutting a purse.

[*While* COKES *listens to the song,* EDGWORTH *gets up to him, and tickles
him in the ear with a straw twice, to draw his hand out of his pocket.*]

Youth, youth, thou hadst better been starved by thy nurse,
Than live to be hanged for cutting a purse.

[EDGWORTH *now has* COKES' *purse.*]

WINWIFE [*Aside.*]   He has it! 'Fore God, he is a brave fellow; pity he
should be detected.   10

ALL   An excellent ballad! An excellent ballad!

EDGWORTH   Friend, let me ha' the first, let me ha' the first, I pray you.

[*He slips the purse to* NIGHTINGALE.]

COKES   Pardon me, sir. First come, first served; and I'll buy the whole
bundle, too.

EDGWORTH   Sir, I cry you mercy, I'll not hinder the poor man's profit.   15

COKES   O God! My purse is gone! My purse, my purse, my purse!

adapted from *Bartholomew Fair* by Ben Jonson

• Talk about what seems to be going on in this scene and where you think the
action might be taking place.

• Try acting out this scene. In addition to the named characters, you will also
needs Cokes' sister who doesn't say anything and a number of people to make up
a crowd. The crowd are supposed to think that Nightingale is there to sing and
sell his songs but of course it is just a trick to bring people together so that his
partner, Edgworth, can rob them. Cokes is a fool who thinks he is too clever to
be robbed and is showing off to his sister. Isn't there an enjoyment for us in seeing big-heads getting their comeuppance?

In a way, this extract shows a **play within a play** – the song is the show and the
crowd are the audience, but in the theatre there is another audience watching

the whole thing. So, while the crowd on stage are taking Nightingale's song seriously, the theatre audience, like Winwife who talks directly to them, are enjoying watching Edgworth get away with the crime.

● The scene is another example of dramatic irony – the theatre audience can see something that the characters on stage cannot. This can be used for comedy or building up tension and horror. Which do you think it is used for here, and how can you play out the scene to make sure that the audience do see exactly what is going on?

● So, how is the audience in the theatre being positioned? Does the playwright want us to see cutpurses (pickpockets) as evil people, or is he actually making a rather different point about them? What do you think?

Unit 20   Playing with the illusion

This is how Peter Nichols' play *A Day in the Death of Joe Egg* starts.

[*Bri comes on without warning. Shouts at audience.*]

BRI   That's enough! [*Pause. Almost at once, louder.*] I said enough!

[*Pause. Stares at audience.*]

Another word and you'll all be here till five o'clock. Nothing to me, is it? I've got all the time in the world. [*Moves across without taking his eyes off them.*] I didn't even get to the end of the corridor before there was such a din all the other teachers started opening their   5
doors as much as to say what the hell's going on there's SOME-
BODY'S TALKING NOW! [*Pause, stares again, like someone facing a mad dog.*] Who was it? You? You, Mister Man? . . . I did not *accuse* you, I *asked* you. Someone in the back row. [*Stares dumbly for some seconds. Relaxes, moves a few steps. Shrugs.*] You're the losers, not me.   10
Who's that? [*Turns on them again.*] Right – hands on heads! Come on, that includes you, put the comb away. Eyes front and sit up. All of you, sit up! [*Puts his own hands on his head for a while, watching for a move, waiting for a sound, then takes them down. Suddenly roars.*]
Hands on head and eyes front! YOU I'm talking to! You'll be *tired*   15
by the time I've finished. Stand on your seat. And keep your hands on your heads. Never mind what's going on outside, that joker at the back. Keep looking out here. Eyes front, hands on heads.

75

Peter Nichols seems to want the audience to believe that they are students in a classroom here – or does he?

● Go through the extract again looking for all those words and phrases that are positioning the audience as Bri's class.

● Now look for all the things that Bri says that would remind the audience that they are, in fact, in a theatre (bear in mind what the inside of most theatres look like and what time of day most plays start).

● How do you think the audience might react to Bri talking to them like this? Why?

Watch out for those moments in plays when the playwright is deliberately reminding you that you are watching a play and not real life, when they are deliberately breaking the illusion. Here are a few moments from plays when the playwright recognises the audience is watching in order to gain a laugh:

PLAYER   We ransomed our dignity to the clouds, and the uncomprehending birds listened. [*He rounds on them.*] Don't you see?! We're *actors – we're the opposite of people!* [*They recoil nonplussed, his voice calms.*] Think, in your head, *now*, of the most . . . *private* . . . *secret* . . . *intimate* thing you have ever done secure in the knowledge   5
of its privacy . . . [*He gives them – and the audience – a good pause.* ROS *takes on a shifty look.*] Are you thinking of it? [*He strikes with his voice and his head.*] Well, I saw *you* do it!

from *Rosencrantz and Guildenstern Are Dead* by Tom Stoppard

VLADIMIR [*Looking around.*]   You recognise the place?
ESTRAGON   I didn't say that.
VLADIMIR   Well?
ESTRAGON   That makes no difference.
VLADIMIR   All the same . . . that tree [*Turning towards the auditorium.*]   5
. . . that bog.

from *Waiting for Godot* by Samuel Beckett

VLADIMIR   We're surrounded! [ESTRAGON *makes a rush towards the back.*] Imbecile! There's no way out there. [*He takes* ESTRAGON *by the arm and drags him towards the front. Gesture towards front.*] There!

Not a soul in sight! Off you go. Quick! [*He pushes* ESTRAGON *towards*
auditorium. ESTRAGON *recoils in horror.*] You won't? [*He contemplates*   5
auditorium.] Well, I can understand that.

from *Waiting for Godot* by Samuel Beckett

MAYOR   It's not enough that I shall be a laughing stock. Some jack-
anapes will write a play about it! Some half-starved, scurrilous scrib-
bler! Oh, he'll lay it on! My rank! My experience! My grey hairs!
No mercy! The idiots will grin and clap . . .! What are you laughing
at? You are laughing at yourselves!   5

from *The Government Inspector* by Nikolai Gogol

● In pairs, imagine that you have arrived in a strange place and are wondering
where you are and what to do. As you peer out across the audience, what comments could you make that suggest you are in a fictitious place yet really know
that an audience is watching?

A word of warning!
  If an audience is not given a clear signal about what their position is regarding
the action on the stage, unfortunate things can happen. Shakespeare's play *The
Taming of the Shrew* opens with the entrance of the drunkard Christopher Sly. In
one famous production the director decided to have the actor playing Sly enter
through the audience, climb onto the stage and start smashing up the set. On
more than one occasion members of the audience tried to pull him back off thinking that he really was a drunk who had got into the theatre and was impatient
for the play to begin! Do you think that the director intended this to happen?

Unit 21 Stage, screen and radio

Stage and screen

You probably see most dramas on television or film, rather than at the theatre.
Regardless of whether you enjoy watching *Neighbours* or the latest Hollywood
blockbuster you are still watching plays. Generally speaking, they tell a story by
having actors play out the actions and words of fictitious characters. The average length of a feature film is about the same as the average length of a stage
play. Both films and stage plays involve one group of people – the audience –

watching another group of people perform. In this sense they are very similar.

The way the story is told, however, can be very different depending on the **medium** being used. Some stage plays find ways of getting the audience directly involved in the action (think about the 'He's behind you', 'Oh no he isn't/Oh yes he is' sort of trick used in pantomimes). This is much harder to achieve on film! On the other hand, films and television plays can direct an audience's attention to something in a way that plays on stage cannot; for example, the way a camera can give a close up of someone's face so that the audience see their reaction to something very clearly. Actors on a stage might give the same kind of reaction but there is no guarantee that all of the audience will notice it as they might be looking at something or someone else.

● Look at this extract from the camera script of a play called *Shakers*. Talk about how it is very different from any stage playscript that you've ever read.

Scene 21: Adele's Song

125	1	
	Follow ADELE round bar (poss 360°) TRACK ROUND HER	THROUGHOUT THE SONG WE SHOULD GET A FEEL OF THE NIGHT WINDING TO A CLOSE, PEOPLE LEAVING, ETC.
		3 BARS
		ADELE:
		Just right now I've had enough.
		Don't want to go and get the bus. 3,4
		Don't want to walk up the estate, 1
126	2	And pick up this sleeping thing. 1
	LS ADELE as she climbs stairs & comes to CAM.	Don't want to have to wheel her home. 3,4,1
		Don't want to sit again alone.
		Hoping the phone will ring. 3,4,1

RECORDING PAUSE:

127	5	
	CRANE UP over bill-board to CU ADELE – & UP	

TO HIGH W/A	Just right now I see no light.	3,4,1
	All there is is black and white.	3,4,1
	All we do is drift along.	1,2
	Stuck somewhere we don't belong.	

128	2		
	CU ADELE	Just right now I've had enough	
		I can't go on the going's tough	
129	5		3,4,1
	TOP SHOT of roof through chimneys		
	TRAVEL to BCU ADELE	But when I hold that baby near	
		A smile is worth the wasted years	
		Just right now I've had enough	
		Even though I've had enough	
130	1	Just right now I've had enough	
	Steadicam ADELE off the roof into the bar	But I'll carry on, I'll carry on . . .	
		7 BARS FADE	

RECORDING BREAK

Pretty technical stuff eh? Notice how much information is included here for different people involved in the production.

The numbers on the left-hand side are the 'shot' numbers (e.g. 125, 126, 127), the numbers next to these relate to which camera on the set is to be used. The numbers on the right-hand side relate to the music which is being played.

Here is a key which will help you see the scene more clearly in your mind:

LS   Long shot: the camera is quite a way from the character

MLS   Medium long shot: e.g. waist to above head

MCU   Medium
close up e.g. head
and shoulders

CU   Close up
(usually of the
character's face)

BCU   Big close up

ECU   Extreme
close up

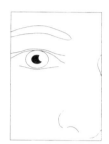

F/U	Fade up
EXT	Exterior: the action takes place outside
INT	Interior: the action takes place inside
2S	Two shot: the camera is focused on two characters
3S	Three shot: the camera is looking at three characters
Track	The camera moves forwards or backwards, often with the character
Crab	The camera moves sideways, often with the character
Pan	The camera sweeps from one place to another
Tilt	The camera moves upwards during a shot to look down on the character
Crane	The camera will be on a crane which can move up to look down on a character from high above
Steadicam	This is a special camera which is self-balancing so that the camera operator can walk with it, following a character perhaps, without the shot becoming shaky
W/A	Wide angle: the camera pulls back to include more of the scene

You will see from this camera script that the audience watching the finished production on the screen will be able to see things that a theatre audience could never see.

Because the audience of a film or television play gets such a different experience from a live audience in the theatre, writers often change the order of the story so that the medium in which they are working makes the best impact.

● Compare the way the stage and screen versions of *Shakers* actually start.

Stage version of *Shakers*

Scene one

Setting: Shakers cocktail bar. The setting is simple in order that attention is focused upon the actresses. A bar, positioned upstage, and four bar stools are all that are used to set the scene. The stools are moved around throughout the action whenever and wherever needed.

During the course of the action, the four waitresses, CAROL, MEL, NICKI *and* ADELE, *switch from role to role, playing the many characters who come into Shakers. Character changes and scene transitions should therefore be punctuated by music and lighting for full effect. In general, music and lighting play an integral part in the play and should be used imaginatively to convey the mood and atmosphere of the various scenes.*

Whilst the audience enters, the actresses stand smoking, clearing away, stacking stools, etc. They address some of their remarks to the audience.

CAROL   I'm sorry. We're closed.

MEL   Yes. We *have* been here for seven hours.

NICKI   Don't remind me.

CAROL   You should have come earlier, love.

ADELE   Sorry.   5

NICKI   It's one o'clock in the bloody morning. What do they think we are?

MEL   It's because we're in the main street. You always get them, especially at weekends, trying to get a last drink as they're passing on the way to the taxi rank.   10

CAROL   Yes.

ADELE   It's because the lights are always on.

NICKI   Stupid that. Wastes electricity.

CAROL   Supposed to make it look classy.

NICKI   What a laugh.   15

MEL   Well, I'm off in a minute. I'm knackered.

ADELE   Day off tomorrow though.

CAROL   But it'll soon be Monday.

MEL   Oh, don't.

Screen version of *Shakers*

Scene 1: Int. Cocktail Bar. Night.

55	5	/0 tape/

Fill frame with steps – CRANE UP steps to reveal LS WAITRESSES continue into V. TIGHT 4-s	PRE-OPENING OF COCKTAIL BAR.
	PREPARATION TIME.
	FOLLOWING VERSES HAVE MUSICAL ACCOMPANIMENT.
	ADELE:
	Ladies and gentlemen, welcome to Shakers
	That trendy place in the main street,
	Where the neon light . . . shines into the night,
	NICKI:
	Tempting passersby.
	MEL:
	That place where dreams come true,
	CAROL:
	Where time stands still,
	ADELE:
	Where everyone wants to be seen From the checkout girl . . . To the chinless yuppies.

(BREAK NEXT)

- Talk about:
  how the set for each production might be different
  the way the audience are included in the action
  the way music and lighting might be used to capture the atmosphere.
- Part of the skill of writing for film or television is to be able to tell a lot of the story through pictures alone. Look back at the example of Scene 21 of *Shakers*. Talk about what impression we get of Adele and her life when we match the words of the song to what the camera is showing us. For example, why does the writer want the camera to take us on a journey through chimneys and roofs to a close up of Adele?
- The choice of camera shot is very important in helping the audience build a meaning for the play and understanding what the character is like. Talk about what impression we would get of Adele and her life if the camera was:
  just showing her face in close up for the whole song
  showing her moving around the nightclub working, in a long shot.

Film directors especially use **storyboards** to record their ideas for shooting the film. You don't have to be a brilliant artist to do this; the picture shows who or what is in the camera shot, and the caption underneath describes the shot in more detail, and says what is on the soundtrack.

Here is an adapted version of the opening scene of Nick Dear's play *Pure Science* and an example of how it could be storyboarded. Perkins is an encyclopaedia salesman whose arrival heralds a dramatic, if gruesome, change in Harold's and Mary's lives.

[*Just before dawn.* MARY, *an elderly woman, sits in the kitchen in her dressing gown. Her husband* HAROLD *can be seen in the garden in his work clothes, poring over a dusty ledger in the first streaks of grey light from the east.*]

MARY   Talk, talk, talk.
Talk blooming talk.
It's all talk.
All night long.
What will become of it?   5
HAROLD   Page four hundred and nine:

[THE BOOK *has a voice; it reads itself to* HAROLD.]

THE WORDLESS BOOK   The copper man gives and the watery stone
receives; the metal gives and the plant receives; the stars give and
the flowers receive; the sky gives and the earth receives; the thun-

derclouds give the fire that darts from them. For all things are inter- 10
woven . . .

HAROLD   Ah, yes, yes, yes, I am getting
the hang of it now.

MARY   In the tiny still part of the night
my husband works at his science.   15
I sit here in the kitchen with my tea and biscuit . . .
For our unremarkable lives are drawing to an end.

CU Mary pouring water into cup

Dawn breaking over suburban skyline.
Fade in Wordless Book: 'The copper man
gives and the watery stone receives . . .'

Tilt down. Close in on Harold's back. He is holding a huge book. Voice: 'the metal gives and the plant receives . . .'

Pull back. Mary watches Harold through kitchen window. Mary: 'Talk, talk, talk.'

CU Mary as she turns her back to window.

CU Cup being stirred. Mary: 'What will become of it?'

ECU Cup being stirred. Fade in Harold: 'Page 409 . . .'

Cup transforms into a crucible being stirred. Wordless Book: 'The sky gives and the earth receives . . .'

CU Perkins looking at house. Wordless Book: 'The thunderclouds give the fire that darts from them . . .'

CU Harold with book. Harold: 'Ah, yes, yes, yes, I am getting the hang of it now.'

Move in on Mary. Mary: 'In the tiny still part of the night my husband works at his science. I sit here . . .'

CU Perkins closing in on front door. Mary: 'For our unremarkable lives are drawing to an end . . .'

- On your own, or as a whole class, watch a clip from a film or TV drama. The clip should not be more than three or four minutes. Try to list:
    all the different types of shots that are used in the scene
    all the different camera movements.
- Talk about what effect was being gained by using the camera in this way.
- Look at the template for a storyboard on page 88. Think of a well-known story – it could be something very simple such as a fairy tale – and draw a template like this of your own, then use it to show how you could tell a section of the story through pictures alone. You might want to experiment with giving the audience a new perspective on the story, that is, telling it in such a way that will make them think about the characters as they have never done before. Remember that when you are doing a storyboard, the square should contain a sketch of what appears on the screen and the box underneath should contain additional information, including:
    what sort of camera shot it is
    what the audience will hear on the soundtrack.

Radio

Just as writers in film and television try to use pictures to tell as much of the story as possible so, obviously, writing for the radio means you have to rely on words and sounds.

Here is an extract from Cara May's play *First Come, First Served*.

---

1 HARRY   If you'll hang on, I'll just unlock the door for you.
2 FX   ENTRANCE OF DEATH
3 DEATH   Jones. Hullo Jones!
4 JONES   [*Interior.*]   Ah. It's you.
5 DEATH   Yes, Doctor, me. Death.
6 JONES   [*Interior.*]   I've been looking forward to this. The Minister and Mr er . . . They've both fine new hearts. Years of life in them.
7 DEATH   No Jones.
8 JONES   There they are. You can see for yourself. Fit as fiddles, the pair of them. A defeat for you! A victory for medicine! You can't deny it.
9 DEATH   I said three months.
10 JONES   84 days precisely, wasn't it. Well, your time is up –
11 FX   DEATH MOVING IN
12 DEATH   Not quite. Any second now.
13 JONES   Fit as fiddles, the pair of them.
14 HARRY   The door seems jammed – ah there.
15 FX   BOMB EXPLOSION
16 FX   FADE IN AMBULANCE SIRENS. HOLD. FADE OUT UNDER
17 JONES   [*Interior.*] That's not fair! You fiend! That's not fair.
18 DEATH   The trouble is, Doctor, you assume I'm playing the game by the same rules as you.
19 FX   BRING UP AMBULANCE – FADE
20 VOICE   [*Fade in on intercom.*]   Attention please. Friends and relatives enquiring about victims of the bomb incident should proceed to Room one nine. Thank you.
21 NURSE   This way, Mrs Jackson. Through here.
22 FX   FOOTSTEPS IN CORRIDOR

● What sort of sound effect would you use to tell the audience that the character Death has just entered?
● How could you signal that Death was 'moving in'?

• Some of Jones' lines have to be 'interior'. Perhaps the writer wants to give us the impression that Jones' conversation with Death can't be heard by anyone else. What would you do with the sound to suggest that this isn't an ordinary, everyday conversation?

• Notice how the scene bounces around very quickly. Jones and Death start by talking to each other. We hear a bomb go off just after Harry forces a door open. Then we hear sirens. Next Jones and Death are talking again – are they in the same place? Finally, we hear an announcement about bomb victims and the scene appears to have changed to a hospital. Perhaps this all sounds very complicated. There are a lot of gaps in the story – but how hard was it for you to understand what was happening in this scene even though you don't know the rest of the play?

• What problems would you have if you tried to perform this script on a stage? Try it, and work out how you might change things in order to make it work.

• Try to rewrite the scene to make it suitable for film (or use the storyboard technique).

Using sound effects can be good fun. Read the script below. You could try to record it with all the appropriate effects or perhaps just make the noises as a class while one of you reads it aloud.

Toby Farnham, crouched over the wheel of his TR 2, was not enjoying the ride. Visibility was down to a few yards as the fog arched its back against the windscreen like a fat grey weasel. Outside a distant church clock chimed midnight but the only sound he could hear was the steady hum of his finely tuned engine and the incessant swish of the windscreen   5
wipers. He'd never make London at this rate . . .

'What a damned fool I've been,' he muttered to himself, 'I should have left hours earlier.'

In an attempt to dispel his gloom, Toby switched on the car radio. His mind drifted back to the weekend he'd just spent. Houseparty at the   10
Hursts'. Boring old lot, except for Jilly, she'd brightened it up no end. He whistled, almost contentedly. Suddenly, and without warning, the car spluttered to a halt. He cursed softly to himself.

'Running out of petrol at this time of night! In filthy weather and in the middle of nowhere! What foul luck!'   15

He switched off the ignition, the windscreen wipers and the radio. Rather than sit all night imprisoned in his car he decided to brave the elements for a while in the hope of finding a garage, even a farmhouse. Anything. He took a deep breath and got out.

The fog leapt upon him, its paws on his shoulders, clinging to him, 20
pushing its cold tongue into his nose and ears. He stumbled on blindly.
'What a pea-souper!'
The only sounds he could hear were his own muffled footsteps and the
occasional hoot of a distant owl. He was just on the point of giving up
and resigning himself to a lonely night in the car when straight ahead he 25
could dimly make out the blurred outline of a building. Too big for a farm
house. Manor house more like, even some sort of a church. No lights on
anywhere.
He groped along the outside looking for an entrance. He found it. A
heavy wooden door slightly ajar. Putting his left shoulder to it, he pushed 30
and pushed. It creaked slowly open.
He was in just in time when the door clanged shut behind him.
Strangely, there was no handle on the inside. It was pitch black and
wherever he was, he was locked in. He cursed softly to himself.
Unable to see anything in the eerie blackness he shuffled forward like 35
a blindfolded two year old wearing his father's shoes. His left elbow
brushed against something cold and hard. And then he heard it. The
laughter, cruel, bloodcurdling. He turned around and as he did collided
into what seemed like a column. A werewolf howled. He turned and ran.
Footsteps echoed after him. Thunder rumbled all around. The wind 40
roared. He crashed into a wall. There could be no escape. In his mind's
eye, he saw the Thing coming towards him. Half man, half beast, half
pissed. Panic stricken, he dug his fingernails into the wall. A headless
rider on a ghostly horse galloped into view followed by a horde of Indians
hotly pursued by the 14th Cavalry. The 7.55 to St Pancras, dead on time, 45
rattled through.
Hands over his ears he screamed, 'Stop, stop, stopppppp!'
And that was how they found him next morning, dead, in the sound
effects department of Broadcasting House . . .

Roger McGough

Section three   Understanding stage directions

Section summary

Stage directions are crucially important in a playscript as they are the clearest indicators of how the piece will look in performance. All too often there is a temptation to skip over the stage directions in the assumption that just following what is being said by the characters will convey the plot. The eight units included here point out the different functions of stage directions and help students come to understand how they work and how their enjoyment of the script may be enhanced by considering them carefully.

22   *If in doubt, read the instructions!*

This introductory unit demonstrates how ignoring the stage directions can lead to complete confusion for the reader by using a short extract from David Storey's play *Home*. The unit goes on to show how different directions are addressed to different people who will be involved in the production process.

23   *Directions in the dialogue*

One of the hardest aspects of reading some plays is that the dialogue itself carries a number of stage directions. Here, an extract from Oliver Goldsmith's *She Stoops to Conquer* encourages students to use their visual imagination to understand more clearly how the dialogue should be staged.

24   *Addressing the actor*

This is the first of five closely linked units which look at who the playwright is speaking to through the use of stage directions and what the production outcomes might be. In this unit extracts from Arthur Miller's *The Crucible*, Nick Dear's *Pure Science* and a number of snippets from Shakespeare illustrate how the playwright gives an actor the key to a character.

25   *Addressing the set designer*

Extracts from *Waiting for Godot* by Samuel Beckett, *Blood Wedding* by Lorca and

Saved by Edward Bond are used to illustrate how sets and the spaces in which plays are performed carry their own meaning.

26   Directions for lighting

Here again, the focus is on how lights are used not only to illuminate the actors but to convey meaning deliberately.

27   Directions for sound

As with lighting, sound may be used to achieve both functional and symbolic roles. An extract from Chekhov's *The Cherry Orchard* illustrates this.

28   Music

An extract from Joe Orton's *The Erpingham Camp* encourages the students to consider how well-chosen music can be used to create dramatic irony and add another layer of meaning to the play in performance.

29   Putting it all together

This is essentially an extension task to the preceding sheets in which the students are asked to consider how set, lights, sound and music might be used to support the actors playing a scene from Tourneur's *The Revenger's Tragedy*.

Unit 22   If in doubt, read the instructions!

Imagine trying to make a model aeroplane from a kit without the instructions. You'd probably get the wings and the body and the other main pieces in the right place and the end result would probably look like an aeroplane. But what about all those other fiddly bits that would make it look like one particular aeroplane? You'd probably have to leave them in the box!

The stage directions in a play give different people details about how the play should look when it is put onto the stage. There is usually still quite a lot of work to be done by directors, designers and actors to work out exactly how they are going to do the job, but without some instructions from the writer they really would be rather lost if all they had to go on was what the characters were saying.

Look at this example from David Storey's play *Home*. The stage directions have been left out.

JACK   By Jove . . .
HARRY   Cotton.
JACK   Oh. Picked it up . . .
HARRY   See you've come prepared.
JACK   What? . . . Oh.   5
    Best to make sure.

Now here is the same extract with David Storey's stage directions put back in:

JACK   [*Reading again.*]   By Jove . . . [*He shakes his head.*]

    [HARRY *leans over and removes something casually from* JACK's *sleeve.*]

HARRY   Cotton.
JACK   Oh. Picked it up . . . [*He glances round at the other sleeve, then
    down at his trousers.*]
HARRY   See you've come prepared.   5
JACK   What? . . . Oh.

    [HARRY *indicates* JACK's *pocket.* JACK *takes out a folded plastic mac, no
    larger, folded, than his hand.*]

    Best to make sure.

It makes more sense now, doesn't it? Without the stage directions here, we, as readers, wouldn't know what was going on. If we were directing or acting in the play, we wouldn't know how to present the scene on stage.

● Read the following stage directions and decide who you think they are addressed to.

A

There are groups of prisoners scattered around the dimly lit edges of the stage.

from *Moll Flanders* by Claire Luckham

B

In front of the fire – since that is the post of vantage, stands at this moment Major Booth Voysey. He is the second son, of the age that it is necessary for a Major to be, and of an appearance that many ordinary Majors in ordinary regiments are. He went into the army because he thought it would be like a schoolboy's idea of it . . . he stands astride,   5 hands in pockets, coat-tails through his arms, cigar in mouth, moustache bristling.

from *The Voysey Inheritance* by Harley Granville Barker

C

The framework of a giant Tipi forms the entire setting. Eight struts meeting in the middle with a larger gap at the front . . . The circular floor, of canvas and an Indian motif, is padded to allow for physical work and acrobatics. In the background hangs a large circular white disc, which can be lit from behind to create moonlight, sunset, day etc.   5

from *Hiawatha* by Michael Bogdanov

D

. . . echoes. Then from behind them a great ripping of ice and creaking iron. The sound of the Soviet ice-breaker.

from *Whale* by David Holman

E

The place is dimly lit by a flickering gaslight high upon one wall, which casts deep fitful shadows across the floor.

from *Sherlock Holmes and the Limehouse Horror* by Philip Pullman

F

She wears a skimpy ochre top and short skirt. A long, narrow, rectangular, white cotton apron, hangs from the neck to her thighs. It is embroidered with a blue border, and decorated with strings of white beads. Her headdress is a high, fan-shaped, brown busby with a coloured head-band sewn with white beads.

from *In Search of Dragon's Mountain* by Toeckey Jones

G

His face has been subtly whitened, to deaden and mask the face. He is half clown, half this year's version of bovver boy. The effect is calculatedly eerie, funny and chill.

from *Comedians* by Trevor Griffiths

● Copy out the grid below. Fill it in by putting the letter of each stage direction against the person you think it is addressed to. You may decide that a number of people need to pay attention to the stage direction, in which case you should put them in order of importance.

Actors							
Set designer							
Lighting designer							
Director							
Make-up							
Costume							
Sound engineer							

● Write a short piece of dialogue of your own which would only make sense if the actors took notice of the stage directions given to them.
● Choose one of the pictures on page 97. Write a stage direction for each of the following which would:
    give a set designer some idea of the scenery she should make
    help a costume designer get the period and style right
    help the actors choose the right kind of make-up.

● Write a brief description of a scene in which sound and lighting would be extremely important in setting the mood and atmosphere.

Unit 23   Directions in the dialogue

When you are reading a play you can't always rely on the writer to give clear stage directions to tell you what they intend to happen on stage. In fact, many playwrights would not want to state too strongly what such things as the set and costumes should look like; nor do they even know exactly how some of the effects they'd like could be achieved technically. They are often happy to rely on the expertise of designers and directors to make the thing work. Including too many stage directions could also make the play difficult to read. They might get in the way of what the writer really wants to focus on, which is the characters.

Often actors, designers and directors can get a good idea of what is necessary to make sense of a scene just by reading what the characters are actually saying. Read this extract from Oliver Goldsmith's play *She Stoops to Conquer*:

MRS HARDCASTLE   Oh, Tony, I'm killed. Shook. Battered to death. I shall never survive it. That last jolt that laid us against the quickset hedge has done my business.

TONY   Alack, mamma, it was all your own fault. You would be for run-ning away by night, without knowing one inch of the way.   5

MRS HARDCASTLE   I wish we were at home again. I never met so many accidents in so short a journey. Drenched in the mud, overturned in a ditch, stuck fast in a slough, jolted to a jelly, and at last to lose our way. Whereabouts do you think we are, Tony?

TONY   By my guess we should be upon Crackskull Common, about   10 forty miles from home.

MRS HARDCASTLE   O lud! O lud! the most notorious spot in all the country. We only want a robbery to make a complete night on't.

TONY   Don't be afraid, mamma, don't be afraid. Two of the five that kept here are hanged, and the other three may not find us. Don't be   15 afraid. Is that a man that's galloping behind us? No; it's only a tree. Don't be afraid.

MRS HARDCASTLE   The fright will certainly kill me.

TONY   Do you see anything like a black hat moving behind the thicket?   20

MRS HARDCASTLE   O death!

TONY   No, it's only a cow. Don't be afraid, mamma, don't be afraid.

● What does Mrs Hardcastle say has happened to her? What sort of mental and physical state do you think she would be in after her ordeal?

● If you were the actress playing Mrs Hardcastle, what words would you pick out from this scene that would help you know how to play the part? Does Tony say anything that suggests how she is behaving? Write a short description of how you might use your voice and movement to show what sort of a state Mrs Hardcastle is in.

● Tony says that they are on 'Crackskull Common'. In fact, the audience knows that he has played a trick on Mrs Hardcastle and that they are only at the bottom of their own garden! (Another example of dramatic irony.) Tony talks about a tree and a thicket being close by. If you were the set designer, would you put these on stage? How about the cow he mentions? What scenery and effects could a designer use to suggest the right sense of place and atmosphere?

● Draw or describe your ideas and write a short explanation of why you have made these decisions.

● Do you think that this extract comes from a serious play? A horror or murder story? A comedy? The actors playing the scene would certainly need to know. Pick out a few lines that suggest to you what sort of play this is, then, in groups of three, try to act it out. One of you should play Tony, one Mrs Hardcastle and the third should work as a director to make sure that the actors are moving and using their voices correctly to get the appropriate atmosphere and style.

Unit 24   Addressing the actor

One of the reasons people find it hard to imagine what Shakespeare's plays look like when they are reading them is that he appears to give very few obvious stage directions. Most of his directions to the actors are worked into what the characters are actually saying. Simply realising this can help you visualise what is going on on stage.

● Read the lines below and, for each one, write a few notes on what you think the actor must do on stage in order to have the lines make sense.

MACBETH   Is this a dagger which I see before me,
The handle towards my hand? Come, let me clutch thee –
I have thee not and yet I see thee still . . .
I see thee yet, in form as palpable
As this which now I draw.   5

JULIET   What's here? a cup, clos'd in my true love's hand?
Poison, I see, hath been his timeless end.

O churl! drunk all, and left no friendly drop
To help me after! I will kiss thy lips;
Haply some poison yet doth hang on them,   5
To make me die with a restorative.
Thy lips are warm!

TRINCULO   Legg'd like a man! and his fins like arms! Warm, o' my
troth! I do now let loose my opinion, hold it no longer: this is no
fish, but an islander, that hath lately suffered by a thunderbolt.

[*Thunder.*]

Alas, the storm is come again! My best way is to creep under his
gaberdine; there is no other shelter here about: misery acquaints a   5
man with strange bed-fellows. I will here shroud till the dregs of the
storm be past.

Some writers go to the other extreme and provide those reading the play with a
great deal of detail about the characters and situation.
● Read this description of a character from Arthur Miller's play *The Crucible*:

Mr Hale is nearing forty, a tight-skinned, eager-eyed intellectual. This is a
beloved errand for him: on being called here to ascertain witchcraft he felt
the pride of the specialist whose unique knowledge has at last been publicly
called for. Like almost all men of learning, he spent a good deal of his time
pondering the invisible world, especially since he had himself encountered a
witch in his parish not long before. That woman, however, turned into a mere
pest under his searching scrutiny, and the child she had allegedly been afflict-
ing recovered her normal behaviour after Hale had given her his kindness
and a few days of rest in his own house. However, that experience never
raised a doubt in his mind as to the reality of the underworld or the existence   1
of Lucifer's many-faced lieutenants. And his belief is not to his discredit.
Better minds than Hale's were – and still are – convinced that there is a society of spirits beyond our ken. One cannot help noting that one of his lines
has never yet raised a laugh in any audience that has seen this play; it is his
assurance that 'We cannot look to superstition in this. The Devil is precise.'
Evidently we are not quite certain even now whether diabolism is holy and
not to be scoffed at. And it is no accident that we should be so bemused.

This is actually just the first paragraph of a piece of writing which goes on for three and a half pages in which the playwright talks about the Reverend Hale's beliefs and compares them to the beliefs he suspects the readers and audience of the play hold. It is almost as if Arthur Miller has suddenly stopped writing a play and started writing a novel or perhaps even a lecture. The question is, does it help the actor understand how to play the part?

● From this description, write a few lines about how you would imagine the actor playing Hale might:

    walk
    speak
    hold his head
    use facial expressions
    wear his clothes.

Other playwrights are more economical in their descriptions of characters but nevertheless help us imagine the type of person they are talking about straight away:

Perkins is a hard nut in a polyester suit. I wouldn't be surprised if his fingernails were disgusting.

from Pure Science by Nick Dear

● Using this description alone, hot-seat a member of your class in the role of Perkins. Ask about his lifestyle, the kind of things he likes, what furniture he has in his house etc.

● In groups, invent three characters of your own which could be summed up in the way that Perkins is. Pass on your descriptions to another group who should then improvise a scene involving the characters.

Unit 25   Addressing the set designer

Here is the opening stage direction of Samuel Beckett's play *Waiting for Godot*:

A country road. A tree.

Evening.

Sounds easy enough to manage. But don't be deceived. What type of tree? What type of road? Will the scenery need to be changed as the play goes on? Will it be evening throughout the whole play?

The job of the set designer is to create an image on stage that is usable and that reflects the meaning and style of the play.

The designer certainly needs to read the whole play carefully to pick up information that might be relevant. For example:

VLADIMIR	He said by the tree. [*They look at the tree.*] Do you see any others?	
ESTRAGON	What is it?	
VLADIMIR	I don't know. A willow.	
ESTRAGON	Where are the leaves?	5
VLADIMIR	It must be dead.	
ESTRAGON	No more weeping.	
VLADIMIR	Or perhaps it's not the season.	
ESTRAGON	Looks to me more like a bush.	
VLADIMIR	A shrub.	10

At the start of Act 2, we are told that:

The tree has four or five leaves.

The fact that the playwright mentions this suggests that it must be important to our understanding of the play. The tree has sprouted leaves – perhaps this suggests new life, some hope on an otherwise bare stage.

● Look at the photograph on page 103 from a production of *Waiting for Godot* and write down what sort of atmosphere it suggests to you.

● Given your own ideas about the atmosphere shown in this black and white photograph, what sort of colours would you use if you were the designer? Give your reasons.

● Use of colour is very important in set designs. Colours have a good deal of meaning for us. Copy out the chart below, and note down any words and images that come into your mind when you think of these colours:

Red	Danger (red flags), love (red rose), blood
White	
Green	
Yellow	
Black	
Purple	

Some playwrights give the set designers more specific instructions about the colours that should be used. For example:

A room with arches and thick walls. At left and at right, white stairways. Upstage, a very large arch, and a wall of the same colour. Even the floor is

103

shining white. This unadorned room has the monumental feeling of a church. There must not be a single grey, a single shadow – not even one required for perspective. Two girls dressed in dark blue are unwinding a red madeja *(a skein of wool). A little girl watches.*

from *Blood Wedding* by Federico García Lorca

● Try to see this scene in your imagination. Even though you may know nothing about this play, what impression would you get from seeing these girls dressed in dark blue, unwinding red wool on a bright white set?

● Try this experiment. Create a performance space in your classroom and place three objects in the space any old how. A chair, a book and a piece of paper will do. Look at the image and talk about what it might mean. Move the objects around. Place the chair on its side. Screw the paper up. Change the book for another one. You will quickly begin to see that once we put something into a performance space an audience will assume that it means something. (Bad news for the stage hand who accidentally leaves a mop and bucket on stage.)

Performance spaces

Waiting for Godot could be performed on an **open stage**. Apart from the tree sprouting a few leaves there are no scenery changes.

The type of stage you are probably most used to is called a **proscenium arch** – you may well have one in your school hall. The arch works like a picture frame, but unlike paintings, stages are three-dimensional so we need a system to know which part of the stage is being talked about. Here is the system we use:

USR	**USC**	**USL**
CSR	**CS**	**CSL**
DSR	**DSC**	**DSL**

——— **Audience** ———

Key:

U Up   **D** Down

C Centre   **R** Right

L Left   **S** Stage

104

Here is a guide to the symbols that set designers commonly use to show things on stage:

Small chair	Windows
Armchair	Open archway
Sofa	Doors (opening on or off-stage)
Tables	Lamp
Telephone	Rostrum with steps 3 2 1
Fireplace (stage right)	

● Use the stage diagram and symbols above as a guide to draw a plan for this stage direction:

_____

The living-room. The front and two side walls make a triangle that slopes to a door back centre. Furniture: table down right, sofa left, TV set left front, armchair up right centre, two chairs close to the table.

from *Saved* by Edward Bond

_____

Even when the designer has decided what is absolutely essential on the set, she will still need to make more decisions. Is there wallpaper? If so, what is it like? What sort of quality is the furniture?

● Read this opening piece of dialogue from *Saved*:

LEN	This ain' the bedroom.
PAM	Bed ain' made.
LEN	Oo's bothered?
PAM	It's awful. 'Ere's nice.
LEN	Suit yourself. Yer don't mind if I take me shoes off?

5

● Using this information, write a brief description of what you now see in your mind for the following things (that is, exactly what sort of table etc.):
table
sofa
TV
wallpaper

The proscenium arch is just one of a number of types of stages. Here are plan views of some others:

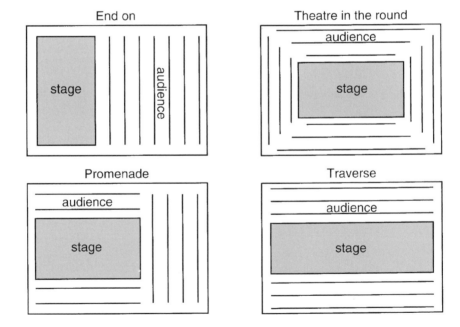

End on

Theatre in the round

Promenade

Traverse

● Not all plays will suit all of these methods. Copy the chart below and fill it in to show some of the disadvantages of the different methods of staging.

End on	The audience only looks in one direction – it can be difficult to surprise them or make them feel really involved in the action.
Theatre in the round	
Promenade	
Traverse	

Unit 26   Directions for lighting

Light is needed on stage for a very obvious reason – without light, you wouldn't be able to see the actors! Because this is such an obvious reason you will find that many playwrights do not give many, if any, stage directions about the lighting. They tend to leave it up to the director to ensure that the play is lit so that the audience can see.

However, the lights need to match the set and the rest of the design. We'd be pretty unconvinced if we saw a play which was set in Dracula's dungeon but was lit as if it was a Mediterranean beach!

When playwrights do give lighting directions we need to pay attention to them because they are obviously important. Sometimes lights are suggested for certain effects – an obvious example would be the use of lighting in a horror story – or to pick out a particular character on the stage.

But lights can also be used to suggest other things. They can take on a **symbolic** value, that is, they add a particular meaning and depth to the story. Consider, for example, a direction right at the end of a play which says:

The stage is bathed in the warm orange light of a late summer evening. They slowly fade to blackout.

● What might such an effect mean if the play has been about:
  a love affair?
  an old person remembering their life?

a young person who is about to leave home?

● Lighting can certainly affect the impression we get of different characters. A simple exercise you might try is to use a torch in a darkened room and shine it on a person's face:

from below
from above
from one side
head on.

Talk about the different effects that are created in this simple way.

● Another simple experiment is to shine a torch on a blank sheet of white paper. Play around with the angle and distance. Try shining the torch through different coloured cellophane (your drama department might be able to lend you some gel which is used to tint stage lights).

Talk about the different effects:

What does blue light suggest?

How about dark blue, orange, red, green?

● Try experimenting with lights by using toy figures or simple figures made from pipe cleaners on a model set. The drama department may have some examples of model sets you could borrow or you could try making one of your own (see the illustration below).

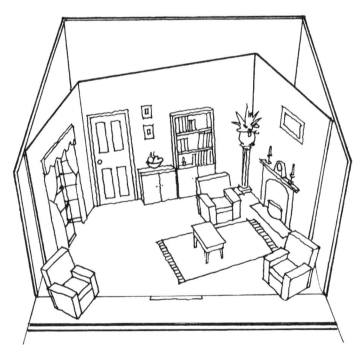

If you are working towards an actual production of a play and have a detailed and realistic model, it would be worth taking photographs of it to show the different effects lights have on the textures and colours and how different shadows might be created.

Unit 27   Directions for sound

As with lights, playwrights tend only to put in stage directions for sound effects when they are particularly important. Many of these are purely functional:

The telephone rings.
There is a knock at the door.

If a character has a line that says, 'Hmm! I wonder who that is ringing on the doorbell,' it would sound pretty stupid if we the audience hadn't heard a ring!
● Some sound effects might suggest something more than what they actually are. Imagine that there are three plays called: 1. *The Love Affair*; 2. *An Old Man Remembers*; 3. *Leaving Home*. What might it suggest if these plays ended with the following stage direction?

We hear footsteps receding into the distance. Silence.

Anton Chekhov's play *The Cherry Orchard* is about an upper-class Russian family who are forced to sell their beloved cherry orchard because times have become harder for them. The play was written in 1904 when life in Russia was beginning to change (there was a revolution the year after). This is the direction at the end of the play:

A sound is heard in the distance, as if from the sky – the sound of a breaking string, dying away, sad.
    Silence descends, and the only thing that can be heard, far away in the orchard, is the thudding of the axe.

● The very last sound effects tell us that the cherry orchard is being chopped down. It signals the end of the pleasant, lazy lifestyle that the family has enjoyed in the countryside. But what about the breaking string? What exactly is that? Perhaps it is more important to consider what it means rather than what it actually is. Discuss what you think it signals.

Right in the middle of the play the family who own the cherry orchard are having a picnic. You need to know that the head of the family is Lyubov, who owns the land. Firs is her elderly manservant. Gayev, her brother, is a bit of a dreamer. Lopakhin is a businessman. He does not come from the same class as the others and is not really particularly well liked or respected by them – however, it is he who ends up buying and cutting down the cherry orchard. During the picnic they all seem quite confident and carefree but look how, in the extract below, it seems that they suddenly turn a corner in their lives.

GAYEV   There goes the sun, ladies and gentlemen.
TROFIMOV   Yes. Gone.
GAYEV   Oh nature . . . divine nature . . . burning with your eternal
light . . . wonderful . . . indifferent . . . – you in whom Life and
Death unite . . . you, in whom the power of life and the power of   5
destruction –
VARYA   Uncle, dear!
ANYA   Uncle, you're doing it again!
GAYEV   Silence. I say no more.

[*Silence, except for* FIRS *muttering. A sound, as if from the sky, far off*
. . . like a string breaking. A sad sound which dies away.]

LYUBOV   What was that?   10
LOPAKHIN   I don't know. Perhaps a cable in a mineshaft breaking . . .
whatever it was it was a long way off.
GAYEV   Might have been a bird. A heron perhaps.
TROFIMOV   Or an owl.
LYUBOV   [*Shudders.*] Eerie . . .   15

[*Silence.*]

Notice how the characters have a very different interpretation of the sound of the breaking string. Lopakhin gives a logical explanation, thinking of something industrial. Gayev prefers something more natural and Lyubov is simply frightened by it although he doesn't know why. At this point in the play the audience may not be able to understand what the sound means, but when we hear it again at the end perhaps we can make more sense of it and understand better why the characters reacted to it in different ways. (Notice also in this extract how there is an instruction for the lighting designer – not in a stage direction but in Gayev's line 'There goes the sun'.)

● Look at the table below which suggests some lighting effects, sound effects and props which might be used to create special meanings.

Light	Sound	Object
coloured, as if through stained glass	gentle lapping of waves	a crushed red rose
dappled green as on a forest floor	a tolling bell	a length of rope
a blue moonlit night	a door slamming	a rucksack
a single sharp white spotlight	a breeze	a telephone
a gentle pink glow	echoing footsteps	an ornate candlestick
flickering orange firelight	sobbing	a large antique globe
bars of grey light	screaming	a crate of beer

● Your task is to choose one thing from each column and write a tiny extract from a play in which they are used to tell a part of a story. For example:

JUDGE   You will be taken from this courtroom to a secure place and thence to a place of execution. And may God have mercy on your soul.

[*The stage darkens. A heavy door slams. Slowly thin bars of light come up centre stage. We pick out the shape of a noose gently swinging from light to shadow and back again.*]

Some of the things, as in this example, seem to go together pretty obviously, but you could have some fun by being inventive and putting things together in surprising ways. It's important that the images make sense, though.

111

Unit 28   Music

Music is tremendously important in drama. Turn down the sound next time you
are watching a particularly scary scene of a horror film and you will understand
just how much music adds to the atmosphere.

Stage plays tend not to use as much background music as films, and often
when it is used it can be, like the lights and other sound effects, quite functional
(the actors in the ball scene of *Romeo and Juliet* would look daft dancing around
the stage without it!).

The choice of music can be used to make a point, though. Joe Orton's play
The Erpingham Camp is about a man, Mr Erpingham, who runs a holiday camp
as if it were an empire. He has a very grand impression of himself which the audience finds difficult to take seriously. Look at how Orton uses music in this scene.

ERPINGHAM   I'll be magnanimous, Riley, and give you the chance of a
lifetime. Seize it with both hands.

[ERPINGHAM *takes a box from the desk and hands it to the* PADRE. *The*
PADRE *takes a sash from the box which he hands to* ERPINGHAM. RILEY
bows his head. ERPINGHAM *puts the sash upon him.* ERPINGHAM *lifts
another box and hands it to the* PADRE. *The* PADRE *opens it, removes
a badge and pins it upon* RILEY's *blazer.* RILEY *is bathed in an unearthly
radiance.*

*Music: 'Zadok the Priest and Nathan the Prophet Anointed Solomon
King'.*

ERPINGHAM *embraces* RILEY.]

ERPINGHAM   Serve us well, Chief Redcoat Riley. And my best wishes
for the task ahead.

[*Music: 'Land of Hope and Glory'.*]

Here, the huge and pompous tones of the suggested music certainly fit Mr
Erpingham's self-importance but do not seem to fit the procedure of giving a redcoat a promotion!

● Can you think of any films you have seen recently where music has been used
to change the meaning of the scene in this way? Describe how the music was
used.

● Write a short scene of your own in which specific pieces of music are used to:

create a particular atmosphere; or
give the audience an indication of what a character is really thinking; or
make a comment on the action (for example, Orton's choice of music seems
to be very sarcastic).

Unit 29   Putting it all together

In the extract below you will see how sound, light and music are all used to create
dramatic effect. The scene is a particularly gruesome one (just count up the murders as you go through!). It takes place in a palace where the coronation of a new
duke is being celebrated by means of a 'masque' (a kind of formal dance display).
The Duke, who is called Lussurioso, is an evil man and has three half-brothers
who all hate and plot against each other. The protagonist of the play is called
Vindice (pronounced Veen-dee-chay) who has suffered at the hands of
Lussurioso and is set upon revenge. He is at the masque armed with a dagger . . .
   Outside there is the sound of thunder and a 'blazing star' which could be a
comet. The thunder and the strange light suggest that something dreadful is
about to happen but Lussurioso seems blissfully unaware of this.
● The scene is very formal in language and movement. After reading it through,
try to act it out (you'll need three sets of four characters):
   Lussurioso and his three flatterers are the audience for the display and should
   sit in a row.
   Vindice, his brother and two accomplices are the first group of dancers.
   The three half-brothers and an accomplice are the second group of dancers.

What happens is that the first group of dancers stab the audience to death. The
second group of dancers come on with the same plan but find that they've been
beaten to it, so stab each other!
   The scene is another example of a play within a play. It's a scary idea, isn't it,
performers starting to entertain an audience then murdering them?

1ST NOBLE   You're gracefully established with the loves
   Of all your subjects; and for natural death,
   I hope it will be threescore years a-coming.
LUSSURIOSO   True – no more but threescore years?
1ST NOBLE   Fourscore I hope my lord.
2ND NOBLE   And fivescore I.   5
3RD NOBLE   But 'tis my hope my lord you shall ne'er die.
LUSSURIOSO   Thou shalt sit next me. Take your places, lords,

113

We're ready now for sports, let 'em set on.

[*Looks at blazing star.*]

You thing! We shall forget you quite anon.

[*Enter the masque of revengers,* VINDICE *and his brother and two lords more. The revengers dance. At the end they steal out their swords and these four kill the four at the table, in the chairs. It thunders. Exeunt all but* VINDICE.]

VINDICE   No power is angry when the lustful die: 10
When thunder claps, heaven likes the tragedy. [*Exit.*]
LUSSURIOSO   Oh, oh.

[*Enter the other masque of intended murderers, the half-brothers* AMBI-TIOSO, SUPERVACUO, SPURIO *and a fourth man, all dancing.* LUSSU-RIOSO *recovers a little and calls out 'A guard! Treason!', at which they stop dancing, and turning towards the table they find them all to be murdered.*]

SPURIO   Whose groan was that?
LUSSURIOSO   Treason. A guard.
AMBITIOSO   How now? All murdered?
SUPERVACUO   Murdered!
4TH LORD   And those his nobles?
AMBITIOSO   [*Aside.*] Here's a labour saved.   15
SUPERVACUO   Then I proclaim myself. Now I am duke.
AMBITIOSO   Thou duke! Brother, thou liest. [*Stabs* SUPERVACUO.]
SPURIO   Slave! So dost thou! [*Stabs* AMBITIOSO.]
4TH LORD   Base villain, hast thou slain my lord and master? [*Stabs*
SPURIO.]   20

[*Enter the first men.*]

VINDICE   Help, guards! Alas, the Duke is murdered.
                    adapted from *The Revenger's Tragedy* by Cyril Tourneur

---

● Go back over the scene and make notes on exactly where you would want to use lighting, sound and music to help build the atmosphere.
● This part of the play, which is close to the end, is very **melodramatic**. It is full of grand exaggerated gestures and is very hard to act without laughing. (How did you get on?) The use of lighting, sound and music will contribute to the melodrama (what sort of music would you choose for the masque?).

Many people are concerned with the possible effects of violence in modern films and television dramas. Has the scene above corrupted you? The question is, what effect would you, as a director, want to have on an audience as they watch these events?

The Revenger's Tragedy was written in 1607 and belongs to a genre that we could call 'horror-tragedy'. Do you think that is an appropriate term for it? It's certainly pretty horrible and probably a bit tragic for those who get murdered (but then again, they were the villains!). Perhaps it is a question of style and how we, the audience, are positioned in relation to the action, and not the violence itself, that makes some people complain.

The names of the characters in *The Revenger's Tragedy* are important. 'Supervacuo' means 'very empty' – in other words, he's several sandwiches short of a picnic. 'Lussurioso' means 'lustful'. But there is more to the characters than this one trait. Supervacuo is violent and dangerous as well as stupid, and Lussurioso isn't just an old lech but very vain. Vindice's name tells us that, although he is the hero of the play, he is also vindictive, that is, consumed with hatred and the desire for revenge.

● Bearing in mind the meaning of the names, what do you think happens after this scene? Does Vindice get away with his crime? Should he? Talk about what message the play would give an audience if he did (or didn't).

Section four   Dramatic characters

Section summary

There has been, in the past, a tendency to look at the characters in plays as if they were real people with a psychological make up grounded in personal experiences which lie outside the confines of the playscript. This section favours a different approach and encourages the students to see characters as constructs which serve purely dramatic functions.

30   First impressions

Here, the students are asked to consider how they come to judge characters in their own experience. A number of extracts from Emlyn Williams' play *Night Must Fall* are used to explore how we come to understand dramatic characters through:

- What they say about themselves
- What they say about each other
- What they actually do.

Other extracts used to illustrate these factors are drawn from D.H. Lawrence's *The Widowing of Mrs Holroyd*.

31   Sub-text

Teachers may most usefully see this unit as an extension task; references are made in this unit to the plays mentioned above. A further extract is introduced from Alan Bleasdale's *No More Sitting on the Old School Bench*.

32   Finding the motive

A number of improvisations are suggested here to explore the business of a character's motivation. These ideas might be used on their own. A reference back to *Night Must Fall* makes an important point about the different experience of reading and watching a play.

33   Characters in action

This unit brings together appearance, speech and action, sub-text and motivation in a structured improvisation and in consideration of an extract from Shakespeare's *Twelfth Night*.

34   What's in a name?

The students are asked to consider what clues playwrights give an audience about their characters by selecting their names carefully. This is related to the device of caricature.

35   Stereotypes

Short extracts from the Capeks' *The Insect Play* are used to illustrate how stereotypes can be used as a kind of short cut to a play's underlying meaning. Reference is made to stereotyped characters in a science fiction play called *Rocket to the Moon*.

36   Personification

Extracts from Marlowe's *Dr Faustus* and Howard Brenton's *Epsom Downs* are used to explain the difference between stereotypes and personified concepts.

37   Functional characters

This unit, although brief, explores the importance to a play of minor characters who only appear in order to move the story on.

38   Cameos

This unit might most usefully be used in conjunction with the preceding one as it makes the point that some minor characters do rather more than simply serve a function to the narrative line. The Porter in *Macbeth* is given as an apposite example.

39   Character development

It's very difficult to explore character development without reference to a whole play, of course, but in this unit an introduction is made to the problem via an explication of the storyline of Mary Morris' *Two Weeks with the Queen* and a number of structured improvisations.

40   Bodies in space

The focus shifts from page to performance in this unit as the students are asked to consider how **proxemics** convey meaning. Extracts from David Leland's *Flying into the Wind*, Noel Coward's *Blithe Spirit* and Willis Hall's *The Long and the Short and the Tall* provide examples of contrasting practical problems.

41   Casting

Attention is drawn here to the effect that an actor's appearance may have on the audience. Two different translations of the beginning of *The Oresteia* are offered, as is an extract from Jack Rosenthal's *P'tang Yang Kipperbang*, in order to demonstrate some of the practical problems of appropriate casting.

42   Costume, mask and make-up

Students are asked to consider what costumes tell us about characters (as well as ouselves!) and how playwrights use costumes, masks and make-up to give information and add effect.

43   Using the whole stage

This is a further exercise in proxemics and explores the difficulties which are sometimes encountered in reading plays in which a number of different things are happening simultaneously on the stage. Extracts from Harold Pinter's *The Birthday Party* and Aphra Behn's *The Rover* provide illustrations.

44   The onstage audience

This unit may be used on its own or as an extension to the previous one. Extracts from Shakespeare's *Julius Caesar* and Willy Russell's *Our Day Out* are used to get the students to consider how an onstage audience might best be positioned so that the theatre audience experiences their reaction to an event as well as the event itself.

Unit 30   First impressions

Are you a good judge of character? Do you make up your mind about people as soon as you meet them, or do you try to build up a picture of what they are like over a period of time?

● Look at the pictures on page 119 of characters from different plays. Paying attention just to their clothes and the general way they look, write a sentence saying what you think each one of them might be like.

● In pairs, talk about a time when you met somebody who you either instantly disliked or liked very much. As you got to know that person better, did your first impression turn out to be correct or did you have to change your opinion because of something they said or did?

● Talk about the ways in which you think you come to know what someone is like.

● We use a great many expressions to 'sum up' what characters are like. A few examples are given on page 120. Talk about what these expressions mean to you. Can you think of any more?

'He's a dark horse'	'I can read her like a book'	'I wouldn't trust him further than I could throw him'

'She's got a short fuse'	'He's an absolute saint'

This unit will focus on a thriller called *Night Must Fall* by Emlyn Williams. Thrillers need to be thrilling; they keep the audience guessing about what will happen next and how. The central character in *Night Must Fall* is called Dan. The audience has already heard a few things about him at the start of the play but this is how he first appears himself:

She is followed by DAN, who saunters past her into the room. He is a young fellow wearing a blue pill-box hat, uniform trousers, a jacket too small for him, and bicycle clips: the stub of a cigarette dangles between his lips. He speaks with a rough accent, indeterminate, but more Welsh than anything else . . . the impression he gives at the moment is one of totally disarming good humour and childlike unselfconsciousness.

• What does Dan's costume tell you about him and the kind of work he does?
• What words in this description of Dan do you find particularly interesting? Jot down three things that are said about him which would make an impression on you, then write a sentence that describes your overall reaction to this character.

What do characters say about themselves?

How would you describe yourself?
• Imagine that you have arranged to meet somebody at a busy station and you need to give them some details that will help them recognise you. What will you say?
• Now imagine that you are going on a foreign exchange trip with your school to stay with somebody about your own age in a different country. The school has asked you to say a few things about yourself so that they can match you up with a partner that you will get along with. What will you say?

● You have applied for a part-time job (you can decide what it is – perhaps helping out at the vet's, working on a children's playscheme, serving behind the counter in a local shop etc.). What can you say about yourself that will make the employer choose you?

So, which one is the real you? Perhaps they all are – in which case, why have you written down different things?

● In pairs, think of a situation in which one character has to say something about him or herself. Perhaps you have been accused of something and you are trying to defend yourself, or you are meeting a new girl/boyfriend's parent for the first time and they want to know a few things about you. Improvise the scene.

● Watch a few examples of these improvisations and talk about:
    what the characters are saying about themselves
    how they are saying it
    and why.

To get to know the characters in a play just by watching it you have to become a bit of a detective. Good! That's exactly what makes many plays (perhaps especially thrillers) interesting. Can you always trust what people say about themselves? People may change what they say about themselves depending on who they are talking to.

Here are a few of the things that Dan says about himself in *Night Must Fall* to another character called Mrs Bramson. She is quite a well-off elderly woman who we always see in a wheelchair.

I know I'm to blame; I'm not much of a chap, but I'd put things straight like a shot if I had any money.

I don't like to impose myself.

I've knocked about a good bit, you know. Never had any advantages, but I always tried to do the right thing.

I don't like to talk too much about my mother. Makes me feel . . . sort of sad.

● What do you suppose Mrs Bramson's impression of Dan would be when she hears him say these things?
● Why do you think he is saying these things about himself to her? You can only guess, of course, but make a note of what you think anyway.

What do characters say about each other?

Another way we come to know about characters is to listen to what other people say about them. Here is what Mrs Bramson says about Dan:

Well, now I come to talk to you, you seem so much better class – I mean, you know so much of the world.

I think you deserve better.

I know human nature, and mark my words, that boy's going to do big things.

Here is what his girlfriend, Dora, says about him:

Dan his name is . . . He's a page boy at the Tallboys . . . he's nice really. He done the wrong thing by me, but he's all right . . . He's funny of course. Ever so open. Baby-face, they call him. Though I never seem to get 'old of what 'e's thinking somehow.

● Do these lines support what you've been thinking about Dan? Or do they make you wonder why Mrs Bramson and Dora might be saying them? They are characters too, of course: can we trust their judgement?
● In pairs, write or improvise a situation in which one of you (A) is trying to persuade the other (B) how nice somebody is. Before you start the improvisation (A) must choose a secret reason for wanting to paint such a glowing picture of this person. Does (B) guess that reason or does she believe what (A) is telling her?

Run the improvisation for a few minutes then talk about what was said that was either:
  persuasive and convincing; or
  gave the game away that (A) had a special interest.

What characters do

Actions speak louder than words. Quiet people may be responsible for great acts of heroism or kindness whereas people who blow their own trumpet might not be able to support their claims with actual deeds. Playwrights must find ways of giving the audience clues about what characters are really like.

In D.H. Lawrence's play *The Widowing of Mrs Holroyd* Mrs Holroyd herself is in an unhappy marriage and is being tempted by a man called Blackmore to leave her husband.

● Read this scene very carefully. Blackmore has brought Mr Holroyd home after finding him drunk in the pub.

BLACKMORE   I think you've said about enough.
HOLROYD   'Ave I, 'ave I? Yer flimsy jack – 'ave I? [*In a sudden burst.*]
  But I've not done wi' thee yet.
BLACKMORE   [*Ironically.*] No, and you haven't.
HOLROYD [*Shouting – pulling himself up from the armchair.*] I'll show   5
  thee – I'll show thee.

[BLACKMORE *laughs.*]

HOLROYD   Yes! – yes, my young monkey. It's thaigh, is it?
BLACKMORE   Yes, it's *me*.
HOLROYD [*Shouting.*]   An' I'll ma'e thee wish it worn't, I will. What
  – ? What? Tha'd come slivin' round here, would ta?   10

[*He lurches forward at* BLACKMORE *with clenched fist.*]

MRS HOLROYD   Drunken, drunken fool – oh, don't.
HOLROYD   [*Turning to her.*] What?

[*She puts up her hands before her face.* BLACKMORE *seizes the upraised
  arm and swings* HOLROYD *round.*]

BLACKMORE   [*In a towering passion.*] Mind what tha'rt doing!
HOLROYD [*Turning fiercely on him – incoherent.*]   Wha' – wha' –!

[*He aims a heavy blow.* BLACKMORE *evades it, so that he is struck on the
  side of the chest. Suddenly he shows his teeth. He raises his fist ready*

to strike HOLROYD *when the latter stands to advantage.*]

MRS HOLROYD [*Rushing upon* BLACKMORE.] No, no! Oh, no!   15

[*She flies and opens the door, and goes out.* BLACKMORE *glances after her, then at* HOLROYD, *who is preparing, like a bull, for another charge. The young man's face lights up.*]

HOLROYD   Wha' – wha' –! [*As he advances,* BLACKMORE *quickly retreats out-of-doors.* HOLROYD *plunges upon him.* BLACKMORE *slips behind the door-jamb, puts out his foot, and trips* HOLROYD *with a crash upon the brick yard.*]

MRS HOLROYD   Oh, what has he done to himself?   20

BLACKMORE [*Thickly.*]   Tumbled over himself.

● Does your opinion about Blackmore change at all in this scene? Can you explain why?

● What problems would this scene create for a director in terms of where the characters need to be positioned and what they need to look like? For example, would the scene work if Mrs Holroyd actually saw Blackmore trip her husband up? Would her opinion of Blackmore be different if she saw his face 'light up' just before Holroyd charged him?

● You might like to try and rehearse this scene in groups of three in order to find out how the audience can be shown something which Mrs Holroyd must not see herself.

So let's take a look at some of the things Dan does in *Night Must Fall* that could help the audience shape their opinion of him:

Wait a minute . . . [*Putting his hat on the table and going to her.*] Are you sure you're quite comfortable like that? Don't you think, Mrs Bramson, you ought to be facin' . . . a wee bit more this side, towards the sun more, eh? [*He moves her chair round till she is in the centre of the room, facing the sun-room.*]   5

DAN   [*Hanging up her rug in the hall.*] Back home again – I put your gloves away –

MRS BRAMSON   [*As he wheels her in.*] I feel dead.

DAN   [*Sitting besides her on the sofa, full of high spirits.*] Don't you be a
silly old 'oman, you look as pretty as a picture.   5

What a nice chap he is!
● But now let's take a look at some of the other things the audience see Dan do,
but Mrs Bramson seems to miss. Mrs Bramson has a niece called Olivia staying
with her. What impression do you think she would have of Dan from this evidence?

He surveys her from under drooping lids, rolling his cigarette on his lower lip.
Olivia is alone for a moment. She stares before her, perplexed. Dan returns. She
looks away. He looks at her, his eyes narrowed. A pause. Studying her, he takes
from the pocket of his jacket a formidable-looking clasp knife, unclasps it, and
tests the blade casually with his fingers. He glances at the mantelpiece, crosses
to it, takes down a stick and begins to sharpen the end of it. Olivia watches
him.

● From this evidence, write a note about:
   what Dan thinks of Olivia, and
   what Olivia thinks of Dan.
● Add this to what you already know about Dan and discuss your ideas about
these questions:
   Why does Dan treat Mrs Bramson so well?
   Why does Mrs Bramson seem to like Dan?
   What does Olivia think of Mrs Bramson?

Unit 31   Sub-text

In real life, people do not always say exactly what they mean or speak aloud what
they are really thinking. The same is true of characters in a play but the playwright must make sure that the audience is given enough evidence to read
between the lines in order to get a full picture of what the character is like. These
messages, which give us clues as to what the characters might really be thinking
or why they might be doing things, are called the **sub-text**. Noticing these
messages, just as a detective notices details that the untrained eye would miss,
helps us to come to our own conclusions about the characters.

In *Night Must Fall*, a young man called Hubert is trying to marry Olivia. He is presented as a rather steady and uninteresting character – very unlike Dan who, as we have seen, seems to have more about him than first meets the eye.

● Look at this piece of dialogue between them where they are talking about Dan:

OLIVIA   It's acting! He's not being himself for a minute – it's all put on for our benefit . . . don't you see?

HUBERT   [*Bantering.*]   D'you know, I think you're in love with him.

OLIVIA   [*With rather more impatience than is necessary.*]   Don't be ridiculous.   5

HUBERT   I was only joking.

● Hubert says he is only joking about Olivia being in love with Dan, but how does the playwright hint that there might be some truth in what he says?

Sub-text isn't always used to show up the devious side of characters or that people are hiding their true feelings because they are vulnerable. In some cases the sub-text creates a good deal of comedy.

● Read this extract from Alan Bleasdale's play *No More Sitting on the Old School Bench*. It's the first day of term in an inner-city comprehensive school and a new teacher, Mr Wright, has just arrived:

MRS SWIFT   Mr Haddock, who is in charge of PE here in the wing . . .

MR HADDOCK   If not throughout the school . . . how do you do.

MR WRIGHT   Pleased to meet you. I did seriously consider doing PE at college as my main course, quite a sportsman in my time, you know, as you can probably tell, it never leaves you does it? But I was finally   5
persuaded otherwise, age really, and my academic inclinations.

MR HADDOCK   What a loss to the gymnasium you must have been.

MR WRIGHT   Yes, I know, but I am still very interested, and I follow all the latest developments, of course. The whole concept of physical education has undergone quite a radical revolution in the last ten   10
years hasn't it? [DEAN *laughs.*]

MR HADDOCK   It hasn't here.

MR WRIGHT   Yes, well, naturally, some people are less adaptable to change, aren't they? [*Silence, apart from* DEAN *trying to suppress a giggle.*] I mean, you know . . . I'm not saying that change is alto-   15 gether the perfect answer, the er solution to all the educational problems, but . . .

MRS SWIFT   [*Taking hold of his arm.*] Oh I do agree, Mr Wright. Obviously a subject for continued discussion – at some later date. Now, here is your timetable, I think it's fairly self-explanatory,   20
although there might be a problem over your room, Room 12, [*Looks at the others.*] but if there's anything you're not sure about, don't hesitate to ask me.

MR WRIGHT   Ah, I see, you're the secretary, I was wondering . . .

MRS SWIFT   Erm, no, not quite, I'm the deputy headmistress, for my   25
sins . . .

MR WRIGHT   Oh, I do beg your pardon, Miss . . . er, I don't know your
. . .

MRS SWIFT   Mrs Swift, and think nothing of it.

MR WRIGHT   I've only met the Headmaster.   30

MRS SWIFT   Yes, I was on a course when the interviews took place. Unfortunately.

MR WRIGHT   A very impressive man.

MR DEAN   Do you think so?

MR WRIGHT   Oh yes, fully in support of the modern methods, you   35
know. Told me so himself.

MR DEAN   We rarely see him down here, so we wouldn't know.

MR WRIGHT   [*Ignoring all.*] There were 143 applicants for my position, you know. 143.

MR HADDOCK   And the Headmaster chose you.   40

MR WRIGHT   I was very lucky.

MRS SWIFT   [*Looks him up and down.*] Yes, remarkably so.

● Mr Wright seems to have a wonderful ability to put his foot in it. Find at least three things that he says here which are likely to upset the other teachers present.

● Some of the sub-text in this extract comes from what the characters are seen to do. Why do you think Dean 'suppresses a giggle' when Mr Wright says that 'some people are less adaptable to change'?

● Why do you think that Mrs Swift 'looks at the others' when she tells Mr Wright that he will be teaching in Room 12?

Mrs Swift: 'I was on a course when the interviews took place. Unfortunately.'

Mr Haddock: 'What a loss to the gymnasium you must have been.'

Mr Dean: 'Do you think so?'

● Look at these lines from the extract and write what you think the characters are actually thinking when they say them.

Unit 32   Finding the motive

Actors often talk about finding the **motivation** for the character they are play-ing. Just as in a detective story, where the murderer must have a believable motive, so, in most plays, the audience wants to understand why a character has behaved in the way they have. If actors are to help the audience come to such an understanding, they have to find that reason for themselves. There isn't always one absolutely right interpretation of why a character does things – different actors and directors will have different ideas.

● Work in groups of three on this series of improvisations, then talk about how the motivation affected the lines and actions. Each improvisation only needs to last for a couple of minutes.

1 (A) is a surgeon, (B) is the anaesthetist. They are preparing to perform a deli-cate operation on (C). Their motivation is simply to do a professional job.
2 The scene is made more tragic when (A) sees that the patient is her husband (or his wife). (A)'s motivation is to try and hold back their personal feelings, (B)'s motivation is to help them both stay professional.
3 Alternatively, it may be comic if, while preparing for the operation, (A) and (B) start to have a lovers' tiff. Their motivation is to try and score points off each other in the argument, while the job becomes routine.
4 Now combine 2 and 3 – in other words, the surgeon and anaesthetist are arguing lovers and the patient is the wife/husband of the surgeon. Depending on how you play this, how you decide each character is motivated, the scene could become very tragic or a complete farce!

The interest in many plays is not to see what happens, but to find out why and how things happen. In *Night Must Fall* the audience are told right at the start of the play that the story is about a murder. In an introductory scene, the audience sees the Lord Chief Justice sitting in a pool of light convicting a cold-blooded murderer. They do not know who has been murdered or who the murderer is – they will have to watch and listen and gather the evidence.

But if you are reading the play you will have no doubts. Here is the full ver-sion of the stage direction for Dan's first entrance.

She is followed by DAN, who saunters past her into the room. He is a young fel-low wearing a blue pill-box hat, uniform trousers, a jacket too small for him, and bicycle clips: the stub of a cigarette dangles between his lips. He speaks with a rough accent, indeterminate, but more Welsh than anything else.

His personality varies considerably as the play proceeds: the impression he gives at the moment is one of totally disarming good humour and childlike unselfcon-

129

sciousness. It would need a very close observer to suspect that there is something wrong somewhere – that this personality is completely assumed.

● What information is there here which tells you, the reader, something that an audience in the theatre would not immediately see?

● Why does the playwright tell the reader this? Doesn't it spoil the play being told that Dan is not what he seems to be? In order to answer this question you need to think about who the playwright expects to actually read the play.

● Why do you think the playwright opens the play by telling the audience that a murder has been committed and the murderer has been caught? Doesn't this make watching the play pointless? What do you think?

● As a reader of the play, do you think you would want to read on even though it's obvious that Dan is the murderer? What would your interest be?

Unit 33   Characters in action

In this unit you will look at how dramatic characters are revealed through:
>   what they look like
>   what they say about themselves
>   what other people say about them
>   what they actually do.

To help the audience form an opinion about the characters, the playwright must make sure that the audience can see why they treat other characters differently and why they are treated the way they are. Through the sub-text we begin to understand what motivates the characters.

● In groups, improvise or write a short play which is based around a character who has recently arrived in a place. Shortly after their arrival something strange happens. Your play must build up a picture of the main character through:
>   what they look like
>   what they say about themselves
>   what other people say about them
>   what they actually do.

You must decide how the character is connected to the strange event. Will you tell the audience straight away what's going on and why? Or will you hide the clues and keep them guessing?

● After you have worked out your play, write a paragraph explaining the decisions you took about how to 'reveal' the character.

● Try out your scene again, but this time speak aloud what the characters are actually thinking when they say some of their lines. For example:

LANDLORD   Well, I'm sure you'll find the room comfortable. If there
are any problems just let me know. (Though I hope you won't moan
like the last bloke did.)

MAN   I'm sure I'll be very comfortable. Thank you. (God! What a
dump!)   5

LANDLORD   Be staying long will you? (No one else has ever managed
to last more than two weeks.)

MAN   I'm not too sure at the moment. I'll see how it goes. (Nosy git!)

In the scene below, which is from Shakespeare's play *Twelfth Night*, there is a
sharp conflict between two characters who have very different temperaments
and personalities. One, appropriately called Sir Toby Belch, likes staying up late
and making a noise. He is the life and soul of the party and loves singing (though
his voice may not be as good as he thinks, so whoever plays this part doesn't need
to worry about being tuneful just so long as he is loud!). The other, called
Malvolio (literally meaning 'ill-will'), is a rather strict, humourless sort who takes
himself very seriously and considers that he is a figure of authority, respectable
and sensible. He doesn't approve of partying.

As you can imagine, the two do not get along very well. This scene takes place
in the middle of the night. Sir Toby Belch is drinking and being rowdy with his
friends in the kitchen of a big country house. It's inevitable that, sooner or later,
Malvolio (who is the chief servant or 'steward' of the house) will be woken up
and come to tell them off.

● Read through the scene and talk about how the characters react to each other.

MARIA   What a caterwauling do you keep here!

SIR TOBY   [*Sings.*]   There dwelt a man in Babylon, lady, lady –

FESTE   [*To* SIR ANDREW.]   Beshrew me, the knight's in admirable
fooling.

SIR ANDREW   Ay, he does well enough if he be disposed, and so do I,   5
too. He does it with a better grace, but I do it more natural.

MARIA   For the love o' God, peace!

[*Enter* MALVOLIO.]

MALVOLIO   My masters, are you mad? Or what are you? Do ye make
an ale-house of my lady's house? Is there no respect of place,
persons, nor time in you?   10

SIR TOBY   We did keep time, sir! [*Sings.*] Farewell, dear heart, since I
must needs be gone –
MARIA   Nay, good Sir Toby –
FESTE [*Sings.*]   His eyes do show his days are almost done –
MALVOLIO   Is't even so?   15
SIR TOBY [*Sings.*] But I will never die –
FESTE [*Sings.*]   Sir Toby, there you lie –
SIR TOBY [*Sings.*]   Shall I bid him go?
FESTE   [*Sings.*] What and if you do?
SIR TOBY [*To* MALVOLIO.]   Art any more than a steward? Dost thou   20
think, because thou art virtuous, there shall be no more cakes and
ale? Go, sir, rub your chain with crumbs! A stoup of wine, Maria!
MALVOLIO [*To* MARIA.]   If you prized my lady's favour at anything
more than contempt, you would not give means for this uncivil rule.
She shall know of it, by this hand! [*Exit.*]   25
MARIA   Go, shake your ears.

● Work in small groups and try to act out this scene and have fun with the
insults they throw at each other. You might find it useful to discuss these issues
before starting to rehearse the scene:
1 What the characters say to each other makes it pretty clear what they think of
each other. But in addition to the words, how can you use tone of voice, volume
and gesture to make it more obvious? How, for example, should Malvolio enter
and exit from the scene? What might the characters do when he exits which
would help show what they think of him?
2 How do you think Malvolio's appearance should differ from Sir Toby's?
3 What do you make of Sir Toby's comment that just because Malvolio is virtuous there should be 'no more cakes and ale'? Does he have a good point, or is
Malvolio justified in complaining about the noise? Perhaps it is the way he makes
his complaint that makes the others abusive towards him.
● Improvise a scene of your own in which a number of young people are being
rowdy and someone comes in to complain. Do they quieten down immediately?
How does the person complaining get them to listen? Try out the scene three
times, with the person complaining using three different tactics to try and
make their point. What different reactions do they get depending on how they
do it?

The case of Iago

In Shakespeare's play *Othello* there is a character called Iago. Othello is a great
general who marries a beautiful young woman called Desdemona. He completely

trusts Iago but Iago schemes against him by suggesting that Desdemona has been unfaithful to him. Believing this, Othello eventually kills his wife who is innocent of Iago's accusation.

The play raises some intriguing questions. Why does Iago do such a thing? Is he jealous? Just plain evil? Has Othello somehow hurt him in the past and he now wants revenge?

Actors will play Iago differently according to what they think his motivation is. But something all actors must remember when they play Iago is that while the audience can see what he is up to, Othello must not. So, do you play Iago as a twisted, sneering, vile creature? Or do you play him as a guy who would be good to have a night out with and share your troubles with?

Unit 34   What's in a name?

It's always very important to remember that the characters in a play are not real. That might seem an obvious thing to say, but it often is easy when you are watching a play (and even easier when you are reading it) to imagine that the lines that are being spoken are coming from real people. That's because in many plays we, the audience, are being asked to 'suspend our disbelief', in other words, to accept that what we are seeing is really happening or has really happened. That's all very well if you just want to be entertained by plays, but if you want to understand how they work you need to remember that every word you read has been selected by the playwright and every action you see has been decided upon by the director and actors – none of it is an accident.

While some playwrights try hard to make us believe that what we are seeing is real, others have lots of tricks to remind the audience that everything they are seeing is invention. One of the tricks they use is in the naming of their characters. Giving a character a particular name can help the audience know immediately what the character is like. When playwrights do this, they are telling us, 'Look, you don't have to be a detective here – just enjoy watching how these people behave.'

- Look at these character names from famous plays:
  Abel Drugger: a tobacconist in Ben Jonson's *The Alchemist*
  Bob Acres: a farmer in R.B. Sheridan's *The Rivals*
  Sir Lucius O'Trigger: a fiery Irishman also in *The Rivals*
  Sneer: a theatre critic in R.B. Sheridan's *The Critic*
  Lockit: a jailer in John Gay's *The Beggar's Opera*.

- What do the following names suggest about these characters?
  Vindice (in *The Revenger's Tragedy* by Cyril Tourneur – you may need to look up the word 'vindictive' to give you a clue for this one)

133

Lady Fidgit, Mr Pinchwife (both in *The Country Wife* by William Wycherley)
Lady Teazle, Snake (both in *The School for Scandal* by R.B. Sheridan)
Mrs Drudge the Housekeeper (in *The Real Inspector Hound* by Tom Stoppard)

● Can you think of any names of characters from books or films that work in this way? Here are a few more examples; add at least four of your own:
Mr Bumble (in *Oliver Twist* by Charles Dickens)
Veruca Salt (in *Charlie and the Chocolate Factory* by Roald Dahl)
Buster Nose (in *Willy the Champ* by Anthony Browne)
Cruella de Vil (in *One Hundred and One Dalmatians* by Dodie Smith).

● Invent suitable names for the following characters:
A man who makes his living by cleaning sewers
A woman who is always envious
A young man who will do anything to avoid a fight
A young woman who is fiercely independent.

Names such as these are often used in comedies – the playwright is telling us not to take the characters seriously. We would say that such characters were **caricatures** – they are rather like cartoons and are often used by playwrights to make a very direct comment about a type of person. Caricatures are often used to make a political point (think about the way impersonators such as Rory Bremner play famous people).

● Look at these caricatures of famous politicians. What does the way they have been caricatured suggest about their real characters?

There is a long tradition of putting 'types' of people on stage which the audience will instantly recognise not as 'real characters' but as representatives of either whole groups of people or as elements of human characteristics. One such dramatic character is actually called Everyman. He appears in a play called *Everyman* which was written in about 1509. The play tells the story of how Everyman is summoned by Death. He discovers that his friends Fellowship, Kindred, Cousin and Goods are unwilling to accompany him. Only Good Deeds, who he has long ignored, is prepared to go with him on this last journey.

● From this information alone, what would you say the purpose of the play is?

Ben Jonson's play *Volpone* is about a cunning old man who tries to trick people into thinking that he is dead in order to stop them getting hold of all of his money. However, those who help him in his plan are as wicked and tricksy as he is. 'Volpone' means 'the fox'. Other characters in the play are: Mosca (the fly), Voltore (the vulture) and Corvino (the raven).

● In small groups, devise a short scene which shows them plotting how to 'stage' Volpone's death. How can you use movement, gesture and the way you speak to suggest the characteristics of the animals their characters are based on?

A more recent example of a dramatic character like Everyman is The American Dream. Here is how he describes himself:

Clean-cut, midwest farm boy type, almost insultingly good-looking in a typical American way. Good profile, straight nose, honest eyes, wonderful smile . . .

The play in which this character appears is called *The American Dream* by Edward Albee and it's about (surprise, surprise) 'the American dream' that everybody should be clean, healthy, wealthy and have the freedom as individuals to do what they want. The audience quickly realises, though, that while the young man who embodies 'the American dream' is good-looking and muscular, he will do anything for money and is really dead inside: he has no real feelings for anything or anybody.

● What do you think Edward Albee is saying about the American way of life by creating a character like this?

Unit 35   Stereotypes

A **stereotype** is slightly different from a caricature. It's as if the writer is using a broader brush to take in a wider section of society. An obvious example would be of a policeman with feet sticking out at right angles, bending his knees saying, ' 'Ello, 'ello, 'ello! What's going on 'ere then?' Used without care, stereotypes can be very offensive, but they can also help the playwright present ideas clearly and directly.

A very interesting and unusual play is *The Insect Play* written by the Capek brothers. In this play, as in *Volpone*, the authors liken certain types of people to animals – in this case insects.

● Read these lines and match them against the type of insect (listed below) you think speaks them:

A

Love me, Clytie.
Visitors are requested not to touch.
Love me, Clytie.
Otto, you're so irresistibly handsome.
I love *you* madly.
I know – I know.

5

B

Our capital – our little pile – our all in all.
Our pi-ile. My gawd – don't frighten me.   '
We oughtn't to roll it about with us till we've made another one,
dearie, did we?
I'll tell you what – we'll invest it – In-vest it – store it up – bury it.   5
That's what we'll do – nice and deep – nice and deep.
I hope nobody finds it.

C

I'll work too if need be, but why should I work when somebody else
has more than he can consume? I've got initiative – but I keep it
here. [*Pats stomach.*] I'm 'ungry, that's what I am, 'ungry, that's a
pretty state of things, isn't it? Anything for a piece of meat, and the
poor man's got nothing. It's against nature. Everyone should have   5
enough to eat, eh? Down with work!

D

The interests of the whole are the highest.
Interests of race –
Industrial interests –
Colonial interests –
Interests of the world.   5
All interests are the whole's.
Nobody may have interests but the whole.

Beetles – who represent small-minded middle-class workers
Butterflies – who represent the upper classes who spend all their time on their
own leisure
Ants – who represent militaristic, totalitarian states
Parasites – which speaks for itself, really!

In *The Insect Play* stereotypes are being deliberately used to make a point about
certain types of people. Sometimes, however, you will come across plays in which
the characters are presented as being 'realistic' but are, in fact, stereotypes.

Sometimes these can give very negative images and reveal what the playwright's personal prejudices are. If the play was successful when it was first performed we might assume that those prejudices were shared by society in general. A well-known example is Shylock, a Jewish money-lender in Shakespeare's *The Merchant of Venice*. Shylock seems to be shown as a man who puts money before everything else and becomes a figure who it is all right to mock. In Shakespeare's day Jewish people were persecuted and had few rights. Many people today feel very uncomfortable about depicting Shylock in this way.

The extract below comes from a play written in 1955 by Neil Tuson. The play is set in the future world of 1987 and concerns a British mission to the moon. In the play, a group of villains try to hi-jack the rocket in order to get their hands on the valuable Trionium which has been discovered on the moon.

This is how the playwright describes some of the characters:

Sir Charles Fitzgerald   He is a tall scholarly man possessing a quiet dignity. Kindly. Elderly.

John Page   Between twenty-five and thirty. Cultured. Thoughtful.

Philip Rosen   A fanatic. But this must not become obvious until he takes control. Once having done this, he delights in his power over the others.

Leslie Smith   Between seventeen and twenty. Very keen on his work and is extremely proud to be associated with Sir Charles and John Page.

Here they are in action:

PAGE   What are you playing at, Philip?

SIR CHARLES   Have you gone mad?

ROSEN   [*There is now an edge in his voice.*] I was never more sane. I am sorry to disappoint you, Sir Charles, but I and several of my friends have a less altruistic and more personal interest in obtaining   5
Trionium than yourself.

SIR CHARLES   Indeed? May I ask what you hope to gain by pointing that gun at us – *now*?

ROSEN   Everything is arranged.

PAGE   [*Stepping forward.*]   Look here, Rosen, don't be a –   10

ROSEN   Stay where you are – everyone! This automatic is loaded and believe me I shall not hesitate to use it!

SMITH   Why – you – rotten little traitor –

ROSEN   I have warned you, Smith, I shall shoot at the first move which threatens to interfere with my plan. [*A buzzer sounds.*] Ah, I   15
was waiting for this. Now then, Smith, open the door!

SIR CHARLES   [*Calmly.*]   Go on, Leslie, do as he says.

adapted from *Rocket to the Moon* by Neil Tuson

Remind you of anything? The stiff-upper-lipped, cultured English leader, the young assistant who seems to have just graduated from the Famous Five and, of course, the power-mad chappy with a foreign-sounding name? You probably won't be surprised to learn that there are two cheerful Cockneys in the crew who say things like 'Cor' and 'Lumme'.

● It is easy now to mock a script like this because it seems so dated, but to what extent are some of these stereotypes alive and well and living in your television set?

● There are no women in this play, but can you imagine how they would be depicted if there were? Improvise a scene between some of the characters in the extract above and a female character of your own invention.

The scene is a real **cliché**, that is, we are so familiar with this type of hero/villain drama that it can seem either ludicrous or just plain boring.

● Can you imagine how this particular play ends? Improvise a scene in which Rosen puts his dastardly plan into action. Does he get away with it?

Unit 36   Personification

Personification is the word used to describe how human characteristics are given to things which aren't human. We are very used to seeing this in children's stories (think, for example, of the characters in the films *Chicken Run* and *Toy Story*).

● Can you think of more examples of stories or films in which things are given a human character?

Playwrights sometimes use personification to bring an idea to life. For example, in a play called *The Spanish Tragedy* by Thomas Kyd, Revenge appears as a character. Christopher Marlowe's play *The Tragedy of Doctor Faustus* is about a man who sells his soul to the Devil in return for great power on Earth. In one scene he is introduced to the Seven Deadly Sins – Wrath, Gluttony, Lust, Sloth, Envy, Covetousness and Pride. Here is how Wrath introduces himself:

I am Wrath. I had neither father nor mother; I leaped out of a lion's mouth when I was scarce an hour old, and ever since have run up and down the world with this case of rapiers, wounding myself when I could get none to fight withal. I was born in hell.

● Choose another one of the Deadly Sins and write a speech that they could make to introduce themselves.
● Now design a costume for your chosen character.

Here is an extract from Howard Brenton's play *Epsom Downs*:

[*The stage deserted.* THE DERBY, *played by one actor, comes on over the hill. The actor is festooned with the regalia of the race.*]
THE DERBY   I am the Epsom Derby Stakes.
Being –
Twelve tons of twenty-two horses and twenty-two small men –
Boots, bridles, crash helmets, weights and whips – silks and light
underwear –   5
Each horse carrying nine stone –
The lot worth twelve million pounds stirling plus –
A race for three year old horses, run over one and a half miles –
Begun over a hill, behind trees, where no one can see a blind thing
that's going on.   10

[THE DERBY *strides over the hill out of sight.* THE DERBY COURSE *comes on. He smokes a cigarette in a long holder, wears a summer suit with two-toned shoes and carries a cut turf in the palm of a hand.*]

THE COURSE   I am the Derby Course. Don't be fooled by lush green
curves in the countryside. I am dangerous. I am a bad-tempered bas-
tard. I bite legs. On me the second-rate burst blood vessels and
heart valves. Only the fast, the brave and the beautiful get anything
out of me. First, I am a killer gallop, up a long hill. Then I sweep   15
down, curving to the left, to the real ball-tearer, a vicious left-hand
corner, Tattenham Corner, turned at forty miles an hour. Then the
straight run to the finish, but down another hill. And at the last
hundred yards – the ground falls away from the Stand into the far-
side rails. That's me. Switchback. Twisty. Feared by the hardened   20
man and animal. To win the Derby – out-think me. Then kick my
brains in. Or I'll break you apart.

● Explain why the Derby Course 'smokes a cigarette in a long holder, wears a summer suit with two-toned shoes and carries a cut turf'. What does this tell you about the real Derby course?
● Choose one of the following things. Write a speech for them and suggest a cos-
tume and perhaps some props they might use:

The Comprehensive School
A Boarding School
Homework
School Dinner
Detention.

● In small groups, decide on something else that could be brought to life by making objects or ideas into characters. Show how they might move and react to each other (you could use the 'school' idea if you want).

Unit 37   Functional characters

Playwrights sometimes need to introduce characters on a stage simply to move the story along. The audience isn't expected to be especially interested in them as characters but more interested in what they do.

● Here are some examples of 'functional characters'. Read their lines and talk about what each character's function seems to be.

SERVANT   My lord, the peasants are outside the palace gate. They are revolting, sire!

MESSENGER   The King comes here tonight.

FLIGHT ATTENDANT   We'll get you boarded, then.

BYSTANDER   He won't get no cab not until half-past eleven, Missus, when they come back after dropping their theatre fares.

Some playwrights deliberately choose not to give many of their characters personal names. In Alistair Campbell's play about the slave trade called *Anansi*, for example, the main characters are simply listed as:
Captain
Boy
Girl

141

Woman

Sailor

Auctioneer.

● In the play itself, these characters seem to be quite real and a lot more than simply functional, so what message do you think the playwright is giving us by simply saying what they are rather than who they are?

● Look down the cast list of some other plays. Look out for characters who are simply listed by their function. Flick through the play to see if you can find what sort of lines and functions they appear to have.

Unit 38   Cameos

A **cameo** is a small but precise picture. In drama a cameo is understood to be a part which, although small, is particularly interesting. A fine example of a cameo role is the Porter in *Macbeth*. Notice that he is simply called 'Porter' – we are not given any background to this character. If he was simply a functional character all we would expect him to do would be to open the door, but Shakespeare gives this character quite a lot to say, although he only appears in one scene. Here is the start of the scene in which the Porter appears:

PORTER   Here's a knocking indeed! If a man were porter of hell-gate he should have old turning the key.

[*Knock.*]

Knock, knock, knock! Who's there i'the name of Belzebub? Here's a farmer that hanged himself on the expectation of plenty. Come in time! have napkins enow about you; here you'll sweat for't.   5

[*Knock.*]

Knock, knock! Who's there in the other devil's name? Faith, here's an equivocator that could swear in both the scales against either scale, who committed treason enough for God's sake, yet could not equivocate to heaven. O, come in, equivocator.

[*Knock.*]

Knock, knock, knock! Who's there? Faith, here's an English tailor   10
come hither for stealing out of a French hose. Come in, tailor; here you may roast your goose.

[*Knock.*]

Knock, knock! Never at a quiet! What are you? – But this place is
too cold for hell. I'll devil-porter it no further. I had thought to have
let in some of all professions that go the primrose way to the ever-   15
lasting bonfire.

[*Knock.*]

Anon, anon! I pray you remember the porter.

[*He opens the gate. Enter* MACDUFF *and* LENNOX.]

MACDUFF   Was it so late, friend, ere you went to bed, that you do lie
so late?
PORTER   Faith, sir, we were carousing till the second cock; and drink,   20
sir, is a great provoker of three things.
MACDUFF   What three things does drink especially provoke?
PORTER   Marry, sir, nose-painting, sleep, and urine. Lechery, sir, it provokes and unprovokes: it provokes the desire but it takes away the
performance.   25

● Describe in your own words what sort of character the Porter is. Think about
what he has been doing the night before and what he has to say about it. Why
doesn't he simply open the gate when he hears the knocking?
● What sort of things does the Porter say and do which seem to make him into
quite a believable character rather than just a functional one?

It is important to remember that every character in a play has some sort of function – the playwright wouldn't bother including them if they hadn't. In the case
of *Macbeth's* Porter it is important to know that the scene immediately before this
one is the nightmarish one in which Macbeth brutally murders King Duncan.
● Why do you suppose Shakespeare followed that bloody scene with this one
featuring a comical drunken Porter? In other words, what function does the
Porter have for the audience?
● On your own, or in small groups, write or improvise a short scene in which:
    one of the characters is a cameo, that is, they are particularly interesting
    because of what they say, though the scene isn't really about them;
    at least two characters represent 'types' of people;
    at least two other characters appear but only have a simple function in terms
    of moving the scene along.
Here are some ideas for where your scene might be set:
    a doctor's waiting room

an airport
on a lifeboat
a school parents' evening.

Unit 39   Character development

Functional characters and cameo roles do not tend to develop through the
course of a play: they are the same at the end of the play as they were at the start
(this is often because they only appear once!).

The whole point of many plays, though, is to show how a character changes
because of things which happen to them. The playwright's job here is to:

make this development believable (in *Macbeth*, for example, Lady Macbeth
seems to go mad – do we believe that she has good cause to?);

signal to the audience that this development is taking place by making
changes to the way the character speaks and behaves.

Here is a summary of Mary Morris' play *Two Weeks with the Queen*:

Colin Mudford lives in Australia with his mum, dad and brother Luke with
whom he fights quite a lot. One Christmas, Luke is taken ill. It turns out that
he has cancer. Colin is sent to England to stay with his aunt and uncle so that
he won't have to be around when Luke dies. Colin refuses to believe that his
brother is really going to die. On arriving in England, he hatches a plan to
speak with the Queen and get her to help cure his brother by providing a better doctor. His antics get him into trouble with his aunt and uncle. They are
reluctant to talk about Luke's illness. One of his plans is to visit the best hospitals in London looking for a better doctor. On one occasion he meets Ted
whose partner Griff is dying of AIDS. Ted isn't frightened of talking about disease, which Colin appreciates. In return, he offers a lot of support to Ted when
Griff finally dies and is actually with them both when it happens. The event
convinces Colin that he should go home to be with Luke when he dies. His
aunt and uncle try to stop him but he has developed into a character that
knows what is right and can argue his case. At the end of the play the two
brothers are reunited.

● Read the following lines from the play. All of them are spoken by Colin but
they are not printed in the order they come in the play. Your job is to put them
in the right order!

---

1   I'm going to have to get into the palace and talk to her myself.
2   You don't understand. I have to go home and be with Luke.
3   I can't face them. I promised I'd make it alright.
4   It was him, he started . . .
5   Alright Colin mate, don't start blubbering. Dad wouldn't blubber. Not even the time you bowled a Malcolm Marshall special off an extra long run up and it bounced off a cow pat and slammed him in the privvies.
6   Why wouldn't the ambulance driver let me in the ambulance? Eh? I never been in an ambulance.
7   I'm going to see the Queen . . . I'm going to ask her to help cure my brother's cancer.
8   I just noticed. Some of them don't look like they're going to die. I mean they look real crook and everything, but they don't look . . . miserable.
9   Mum, stop worrying. You've seen those Sydney hospitals on telly; they got everything. They could cure a horse with its head on backwards down there. Come on, eat your curry.
10 I'm glad he wasn't alone.

The Greeks had a special word to describe the way many dramatic characters develop through the course of a play – they called it **anagnorisis** which means 'recognition' – a journey from ignorance to awareness. Some characters start the play not knowing much about themselves as people. As they deal with things in the course of the play they come to know themselves better. Some characters come to understand other people better through the course of the play because of the way they behave in the different situations. Some characters come to understand a *situation or issue* because of the way they encounter events in the play.

● In groups of three or four, devise a simple story that shows how a character develops in one of the three ways suggested above.

● Show your story in a series of still images (no more than five). For example:
1   A group of youths are teasing a character who looks frightened of them.
2   The character witnesses a young child in a dangerous situation.
3   The character rescues the child.
4   The character is praised by the child's parents.
5   The character is shown walking through the gang of youths confidently.
Rather simplistic, you'll agree – no doubt you will do something much better!

An alternative to improvising these still images would be to draw a cartoon-strip using 'stick-men' as figures. Use captions and speech balloons to help explain what happens in the story.

145

Unit 40   Bodies in space

Have you ever had that uncomfortable experience of someone who you don't know terribly well standing just a bit too close to you? Or how about those times when someone who you thought was a good friend seems to take a step back or turn sideways when you approach?

The way we move our bodies in space tells other people a great deal not only about us as individuals, but about what we think of other people.

● In pairs, try out this piece of dialogue:

---

1   So, back off holiday I see.

2   Yes. That's right.

1   Nice time?

2   Fine, thank you.

1   Good. Now I wonder if we might have a chat about one or two things.   5

2   Do you think we need to?

1   Yes.

2   Yes.

● First of all, try this standing facing each other about a metre or so apart.
● Try again a little closer.
● Try it virtually nose to nose!
● Try it with 1 standing and 2 sitting. What happens if 1 stands behind 2's chair?
● What if 1 keeps moving around?

Positioning on stage is hugely important. Playwrights often leave it up to the actors and the director to interpret for themselves what the **proxemics** (that is, the use of space) should be in a scene.

● Read and work on the following three extracts, which have been slightly adapted from the original.

Flying into the Wind by David Leland

This scene is set in a courtroom. The case is about whether Mr and Mrs Wyatt have the right not to send their children to school. Some of the evidence comes

146

from their daughter Laura who is now 18 but stopped going to school ten years ago. She is being asked questions about her ability to read. The other two characters are the lawyer, Healey, and the chairman of the court, Judge Wood.

HEALEY   Very well, could I ask you to read this article to the court?

LAURA   You are trying to test me. I do not wish to be tested.

HEALEY   This is not a test; I simply wish to establish if you are able to read or not.

LAURA   I can read. I have told you I can read.   5

JUDGE WOOD   The request is reasonable, Miss Wyatt. Mr Healey simply wishes to establish your basic level of reading comprehension. We might then go on to ask how you have achieved this.

LAURA   I have said that I can read, your honour.   10

JUDGE WOOD   Then you have nothing to fear. Please answer Mr Healey's question.

HEALEY   Miss Wyatt, can you please tell the court, and please refer to the magazine article if you wish to, what the article you have before you is about?   15

[LAURA WYATT *reads the magazine article. As she reads, she begins to shake. There are tears in her eyes which she tries to hold back.*]

Laura seems, at the end of the scene, to feel threatened and vulnerable in this situation.

● Try out the scene. How would you position the three characters to show who has the most power here? Whose side do you expect the audience to be on in this scene and why? Talk about:
   the language each character uses
   who they actually are.

● What article would you choose to have Laura read aloud:
   if you wanted the audience to sympathise with her?
   if you wanted them to see her as being a bit pathetic?

Blithe Spirit by Noel Coward

This scene also shows three characters together. Here they are involved in a séance which has gone wrong. Charles, who is married to Ruth, now finds that

147

his previous and deceased wife Elvira has come back to live with them. He can see Elvira (and so can the audience – another case of dramatic irony) but Ruth cannot.

RUTH [*To* ELVIRA.]   I want to ask you a question. Why did you come here?

ELVIRA   I came because the power of Charles's love tugged and tugged and tugged at me. Didn't it, my sweet?

RUTH   What did she say?   5

CHARLES   She said that she came because she wanted to see me again.

RUTH   Well, she's done that now, hasn't she?

CHARLES   We can't be inhospitable, Ruth.

RUTH   I have no wish to be inhospitable, but I should like to have just an idea of how long you intend to stay, Elvira.   10

ELVIRA   I don't know – I really don't know! [*She giggles.*] Isn't it awful?

CHARLES   She says she doesn't know.

RUTH   Surely that's a little inconsiderate?

CHARLES   Don't be upset, Ruth dear – we shall soon adjust ourselves, you know. I can see no valid reason why we shouldn't get a great   15
deal of fun out of it.

RUTH   Fun! Charles, how can you – you must be out of your mind!

CHARLES   Not at all – I thought I was at first – but now I must say I'm beginning to enjoy myself.

RUTH   [*Bursting into tears.*]   Oh Charles, Charles . . .   20

ELVIRA   She's off again.

CHARLES   You really must not be so callous, Elvira. Try to see her point a little.

RUTH   I suppose she said something insulting . . .

CHARLES   No, dear, she didn't do anything of the sort.   25

RUTH   Now look here, Elvira . . .

CHARLES   She's over by the window now.

RUTH   Why the hell can't she stay in the same place?

ELVIRA   Temper again – my poor Charles, what a terrible life you must lead.   30

CHARLES   Shut up, darling, you'll only make everything worse.

RUTH   Who was that 'darling' addressed to – her or me?

● Highlight all the moments in the extract which show that Ruth can neither see nor hear Elvira.

148

- Act out the scene. Think carefully about how there must be differences in the way Ruth and Charles move and behave which would demonstrate that one can see Elvira but the other cannot.
- Is there anything Elvira could do or anywhere she could move that would annoy Charles more and make Ruth look more foolish?
- Improvise an extension to this scene to show Ruth becoming more frustrated, Charles having to be more tactful and Elvira becoming more teasing.

The Long and the Short and the Tall by Willis Hall

In this scene one of the characters says nothing at all, yet he is in many ways the centre of attention. The setting is the Malayan jungle in World War II, and the silent character is a Japanese soldier who has been captured by a British patrol. Two of them, Sergeant Mitchem and Lance Corporal Macleish, are discussing the next move.

MACLEISH   So how does he end up when we head back?

MITCHEM   We're stacking him. He's no use now. He couldn't tell us any more than we know already. He's lost his value.

MACLEISH   Are we going to leave him here?

MITCHEM   Yeah.   5

MACLEISH   In the hut?

MITCHEM   That's right.

MACLEISH   That's a bit risky, isn't it?

MITCHEM   How do you mean?

MACLEISH   Suppose they find the track up here? Suppose the Japs   10
come up and cut him loose? He lets them know what time we left. How many there are of us. They'd catch us up in no time . . .

MITCHEM   He won't.

MACLEISH   There's nothing to stop him.

MITCHEM   I've told you, he won't. They'll find him, that's all.   15

MACLEISH   But he can tell them. About us.

MITCHEM   He won't tell anybody. Anything.

MACLEISH   What's to stop him?

MITCHEM   I'll see to that.

MACLEISH   You're not . . . you're not going to knock him off?   20

MITCHEM   Do you want to do it?

MACLEISH   He's a prisoner of war!

MITCHEM   Shut up.

As you can see, it only gradually dawns on Macleish that the unarmed Japanese soldier is to be killed. The act might seem to the audience to be cold-blooded murder, and we are reminded of this by the way the soldier is silently listening to the conversation throughout.

● Read through the scene in pairs. Try to make it clear in the way you read that Mitchem knows something Macleish does not; for example, look at the line 'He won't tell anybody. Anything.' What difference would it make if the playwright had just written, 'He won't tell anybody anything'?

● Now look through the scene in groups of three, with one of you sitting as the Japanese soldier. Remember, the speakers are talking about the prisoner, not to him. Try out different ways of positioning the British soldiers. The actor playing the Japanese soldier could usefully comment on which positions make him feel more uncomfortable.

● Try the scene with the Japanese prisoner sitting completely motionless as if he understands nothing, then compare this to the effect gained if he acts as if he is beginning to understand what is going on. Which way do you think would be most effective for the audience and why?

● In a larger group, you could improvise the next scene in which the rest of the patrol return and learn what Mitchem is planning. How could you position the characters to show who is with Mitchem and who is worried about what he intends to do?

Unit 41   Casting

When we watch a play what we see is bodies on a stage (or screen) – we don't see the words on the page. This raises the question of what sort of actors are chosen to play the different characters. A film which cast Hugh Grant as Frankenstein or Dawn French as Cleopatra might be a bit hard to swallow. (You could have some fun thinking up other ridiculous casting decisions – the trouble is, some directors make them!)

When Hollywood studios cast films they often want to put big stars in the major roles, and this may be why sometimes the decisions don't quite work. For an actor to fit a certain role, a number of things have to be considered such as age, sex, build and voice. They must also consider what the audience already know about and expect of the actors in films (Ali G as Richard III?).

Sometimes playwrights give us quite precise details in the cast list or stage directions about what sort of actor they want to play a part, but in most cases we have to try to gather clues from the text itself.

At the start of a play called *Agamemnon* by the ancient Greek playwright Aeschylus, a watchman is looking to the horizon for any sign of a beacon which will indicate that the Trojan War is finally over. The beacon appears. As you read through the scene, try to decide what sort of actor could best play the part. It's a male role, obviously, but what other decisions would you make? (By the way, Argos is a place in Greece, not a high street store!)

WATCHMAN   I have made suit to Heaven for release
A twelvemonth long from this hard service, here
At watch upon the palace roof to lie
As if these arms were paws and I a dog.
. . .
Oh, that the hour were come for my release!   5
Oh, for the gloom's glad glow of herald-fire!

[*The beacon shines out on Mount Arachne.*]

Brave lantern! Out of the darkness bringing bright
Day! jolly dance and jocund revelry
To all broad Argos for this fair windfall!
                    adapted from the translation by G.M. Cookson

---

● So, how do you see this character? Young? Old? Loud and dominating, or quiet? Is he important and imposing, or ordinary and bored? Describe what you think he looks like.
● Here is a more modern translation of the same scene. Would your ideas about casting work for this version?

WATCHMAN   No end to it all, though all year I've muttered
My pleas to the gods for a long groped for end.
Wish it were over, this waiting, this watching,
Twelve weary months, night in and night out,
Crouching and peering, head down like a bloodhound,   5
Paws propping up muzzle, up here on the palace.
. . .
Maybe tonight it'll finish, this watching, this waiting.
Come on, blasted beacon, blaze out of the blackness!

[*Sees beacon.*]

It's there! An oasis like daylight in deserts of dark!

There'll be dancing in Argos, and I'll lead the dance!   10
adapted from the translation by Tony Harrison

● Was this watchman different from the first one? Describe the kind of actor you would want to play this part.

Here is a very different casting problem. In this scene, adapted from Jack Rosenthal's television play *P'tang, Yang, Kipperbang*, we see two 14-year-olds – Alan and Ann. They are at the gate of Ann's house, having walked home from school together. The extract comes from quite late on in the play, which is set in 1948.

ALAN [*Looking at her. He speaks quietly, solemnly, completely unselfconsciously, and very, very simply.*]   You're beautiful, Ann. Sometimes I look at you and you're so beautiful I want to cry. And sometimes you look so beautiful I want to laugh and jump up and down and run through the streets with no clothes on shouting 'P'tang yang kip-   5 perbang' in people's letterboxes. [*Pause.*] But mostly you're so beautiful – even if it doesn't make *me* cry it makes my chest cry. Your lips are the most beautiful. Second is your nape.
ANN [*Slight pause.*]   My what?
ALAN   The back of your neck. It's termed the nape.   10
ANN   Oh, my *nape*.
ALAN   And your skin. When I walk past your desk, I breathe in on purpose to smell your skin. It's the most beautiful smell there is.
ANN   It's only Yardley's.
ALAN   It makes me feel dizzy. Giddy. You smell brand-new. All of you.   15
The little soft hairs on your arms.
ANN   That's *down*. It's not hairs. It's called down. Girls can have down.
ALAN   But mostly it's your lips. I love your lips. That's why I've *always* wanted to kiss you. Ever since 3B. Just kiss. Not the other things. I   20
don't want to do the other things to you. [*Pause.*] Well, I *do*. All the other things. Sometimes I want to do them so much I feel I'm – do you have violin lessons?
ANN [*Thrown.*]   What?
ALAN   On the violin.   25
ANN   No. Just the recorder. Intermediate, Grade Two.

152

ALAN   Well, on a violin there's the E string. That's the highest pitched and it's strung very tight and taut, and makes a kind of high, sweet scream. Well, sometimes I want you so much, that's what *I'm* like.

[*A pause.*]

ANN   [*Uncertain.*]   Um . . . thank you.   30

● Who in your class would you cast in the roles of Alan and Ann and why?
● If you were feeling brave and were directing a play for the teachers in your school, which of your teachers would you cast in these roles? Why?

Unit 42   Costume, mask and make-up

Are you what you wear?

What do costumes tell us about a character?
● Look at the pictures below and on page 154 and focus on the costumes they are wearing. Write one sentence about what these costumes tell you about each character.

If you think for a moment about the clothes you yourself wear on different occa-sions you will probably agree that clothes can tell other people a lot about you. It may be that you want to consciously give people a message about who you are. Perhaps you and your friends all tend to wear the same kind of things to show that, well, to show that you are friends! Perhaps you deliberately wear clothes that you know your parents hate – what are you trying to say when you do this? It may be that, like it or not, you have to wear school uniform. Either way, your clothes are a statement about the life you lead and the way you are.

There are all sorts of reasons for us to wear particular clothes. Certain clothes are linked to particular jobs (when did you last see a guy in a wet suit walking down the High Street?) or certain social expectations (ever seen the Queen in a pair of cut-off Levi's?).

● Copy out this chart and add more ideas of your own:

Reasons for wearing different clothes	Examples
Social expectations	Something 'smart' for a wedding
Job	Spacesuit
Status	Mayor's regalia
Because there is no choice	Beggars
Membership of a group	Doc Marten boots

In plays, costume can be used very deliberately to give an audience information about the characters and the world they inhabit. It's another example of why watching a play is a more direct experience than reading it and can make the play much easier to understand. However, if you are just reading a play, you must try to see the characters in costume in your mind's eye.

Pretty obviously, costume can tell us what period or country the play is set in, but the smartness, shabbiness and style of their costumes can also tell us something about the individuals wearing them (just as their voices and the way they pronounce things can tell us about where they come from and what social class they are).

● What is often particularly noticeable is when a character changes costume in a play. Look at the examples below. Why do you think the playwright has suggested the costume change?

1 Lady Macbeth is made Queen after she has helped her husband murder the old king. We see her parading around a banquet looking every part a Queen. But later, wracked by guilt, she takes to sleep-walking. Here we see her in her nightdress. What does this change in costume say?

2 Malvolio is a strict and humourless steward in *Twelfth Night*. In order to tease him, other characters trick him into appearing 'yellow-stockinged and cross gartered'. How does this make him look and what will the audience's reaction be?

3 In Bertolt Brecht's play *Mother Courage* there is a whore called Yvette who wears bright red boots and a colourful hat. Mother Courage's daughter delights in trying the hat and boots over her own drab clothes. Mother Courage sees her and gives her a severe telling off. Why?

4 In the play *In Search of Dragon's Mountain* there is a character called Apartheid. He wears a safari suit and suede desert boots typical of the white supporters of apartheid in South Africa. At the end of the play, apartheid has been abolished in South Africa. The character comes on to speak to the audience but now just wears a long black coat and says, 'You might think you got rid of me in South Africa, but sooner or later I pop up somewhere else.' What is the significance of this costume change?

The colour of certain costumes can be tremendously important. As with stage lights, colours can mean a great deal. Red, for example, can be a very sexy colour – Yvette in *Mother Courage* uses the red boots to attract men.

John Arden's play *Sergeant Musgrave's Dance* is set in a poor mining community in winter. Imagine what the stage might look like – sooty houses contrasting with the white snow in the street. Into this set comes Sergeant Musgrave and his men dressed in bright red army tunics. They look smart and exciting, but the boldness of the contrasting colours also seems to signal danger and blood.

● What other things do you think the colour red can be used to indicate when it is used in a costume?

155

Imagine the interior of a great grey stone castle. All the characters seem noble and wear lavish and colourful costumes – all except one who is dressed in black. What you are seeing in your mind's eye might be a scene from *Hamlet*.
● What effect does his black costume have in this setting?

Not all characters in plays are straightforward representations of real people. In Ben Jonson's play *Volpone* the characters are human but seem to have the personalities of certain animals. One is cunning like a fox, another seems quite evil in the way he picks around like a vulture.
● How could their personality be reflected in the costume they wear? Design a costume for a character that is in some way like an animal and say why you have designed it in that way.

In *The Insect Play* by the Capek brothers the characters are actually animals but seem to remind us of certain types of humans. Look back to pages 136–137 for some examples.
● Describe or draw a costume for one of the characters in the play and explain your decisions.

Which witch?

What do you see in your imagination when you hear or read the word 'witch'?
    The answer is all too obvious – and that's exactly the problem faced by anyone putting on the play *Macbeth*. How seriously can an audience take the witches in that play if they are shown on stage with pointy black hats, hooked warty noses and blacked-out teeth? We are so used to the kiddies' cartoon image of witches that presenting *Macbeth* witches in this way is very likely to make an audience either just switch off or giggle. So, what would you do?
● Brainstorm around the word 'witches'. For example, 'supernatural . . . scary . . . temptresses . . . deceive people . . .' Add your own ideas on a sheet of card.
● Pick out just a few of these words that you might use as the key to how you could present the witches in *Macbeth*, and design a costume that would capture these particular attributes.

Make-up and mask

Everything we have said about costume is also true of make-up; that is, make-up might make a character look instantly recognisable as a part of a group or indicate that they are of a certain age. Make-up can show the character comes from a particular era or place, or it can accentuate an aspect of the character.
    It's quite helpful to see the use of make-up as falling into two categories: 'naturalistic' and 'heightened'.

156

'Naturalistic' make-up attempts to make the characters look like real life people. In fact, audiences will often not even notice that an actor is wearing any make-up. The fact is that stage lighting, and more particularly television and film lighting, tends to make people's natural colouring look odd. Make-up is used to compensate for this. Make-up can also be used by an actor to help them create a believable naturalistic character that is, in fact, completely different to them. There's probably no better example of how make-up can be used to create believable characters than in the film *Mrs Doubtfire* where an out-of-work actor uses extensive make-up to turn himself into an ageing nanny.

● Talk about any films and television dramas you know where an actor has been made up as a wholly believable character that looks completely different from the way they look in real life.

Robin Williams in *Mrs Doubtfire*.

'Heightened' make-up includes a vast range of effects and purposes. Heightened make-up can, of course, be used by real, believable characters simply because it is the fashion. Gentlemen in 18th-century England, for example, would have worn wigs, powder, rouge and lipstick as a matter of course.

Heightened make-up might be used to suggest a particular trait. In Christopher Marlowe's play *The Tragical History of Doctor Faustus* the audience see a procession of the Seven Deadly Sins: Pride, Covetousness, Envy, Wrath, Gluttony, Sloth and Lust.

● How could you use make-up to suggest one of these characters? (Remember that wigs and hair styles are a part of make-up.)

Heightened make-up also includes make-up that is used for symbolic or ritualistic purposes. An obvious example of this is war paint. There are many fascinating examples of dramatic make-up having a highly symbolic value.

It seems only a small step between this type of heightened make-up and mask. Masks have been a part of performance since drama first began. In primitive rituals, for example, men would wear animal masks to re-enact a hunt. Later, in Greek theatre, masks were used to indicate character types. You will no doubt be familiar with the classic depictions of comedy and tragedy which are often used to symbolise theatre.

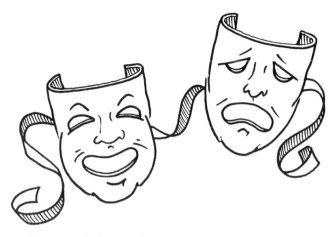

Masks can add a great deal to the dramatic impact of a play. Sometimes they can make us laugh at a character's features or feel sympathetic towards them. At other times masks can be very disconcerting because of the way they 'dehumanise' the characters.

● Look at the masks in the photograph below and talk about the effect they are likely to have on an audience.

Masks used in a production of A Midsummer Night's Dream.

159

Unit 43   Using the whole stage

Perhaps the biggest problem with reading plays is that it is sometimes very difficult to imagine, from the words on the page, what the play will look like on stage.
● Read this extract from Harold Pinter's *The Birthday Party*.

MCCANN   Give me your glass.

> [MEG *sits on a shoe-box, downstage, right.* LULU, *at the table, pours more*
> *drink for* GOLDBERG *and herself, and gives* GOLDBERG *his glass.*]

GOLDBERG   Thank you.
MEG   [*To* MCCANN.] Do you think I should?
GOLDBERG   Lulu, you're a big bouncy girl. Come and sit on my lap.
MCCANN   Why not?   5
LULU   Do you think I should?
GOLDBERG   Try it.
MEG   [*Sipping.*]   Very nice.
LULU   I'll bounce up to the ceiling.
MCCANN   I don't know how you can mix that stuff.   10
GOLDBERG   Take a chance.
MEG   [*To* MCCANN.]   Sit down on this stool.

> [LULU *sits on* GOLDBERG's *lap.*]

MCCANN   This?
GOLDBERG   Comfortable?
LULU   Yes thanks.   15
MCCANN   [*Sitting.*] It's comfortable.
GOLDBERG   You know, there's a lot in your eyes.
LULU   And in yours, too.
GOLDBERG   Do you think so?
LULU   [*Giggling.*]   Go on!   20
MCCANN   [*To* MEG.]   Where'd you get it?
MEG   My father gave it to me.
LULU   I didn't know I was going to meet you here tonight.
MCCANN   [*To* MEG.]   Ever been to Carrikmacross?
MEG   [*Drinking.*]   I've been to King's Cross.   25
LULU   You came right out of the blue, you know that?
GOLDBERG   [*As she moves.*]   Mind how you go. You're cracking a rib.

● On first reading this, you might think it's complete gobbledygook. The dialogue doesn't seem to follow on logically. Why, for example, does McCann say, 'I don't know how you can mix that stuff' straight after Lulu has said, 'I'll bounce up to the ceiling'? Who is she talking to?

● Who is Goldberg talking to when he says, 'You're cracking a rib' and why does he say it?

● You've probably twigged by now that the trick to reading this scene is to realise that there are two separate conversations going on. In groups of four, try the scene out with Meg and McCann being close together in one area, and Goldberg and Lulu staying together a metre or so away.

● Go through the scene again, but this time have all four characters moving around amongst each other. Don't worry about the stage directions, just move around and keep the dialogue flowing, leaving no space between one line and the next.

● Now stage the scene in a polished way. What you are trying to achieve is the atmosphere of a party where lots of people are talking at once over the top of each other and a number of different things are happening at once. You might find that while on the page the dialogue seems bizarre, when it is acted out it becomes naturalistic, almost as if someone had just stuck a microphone into a room where a small party was taking place.

● Improvise a scene of your own. Imagine the scene is a restaurant, or a form room or a pub. Let's call it *Separate Tables*. Work in two pairs: when there is a pause in the conversation, the other pair can take over. If you concentrate hard you should be able to do this and swap backwards and forwards without anyone talking over anyone else.

Now look at this scene from *The Rover*, which was written by Aphra Behn in 1677. It is only quite recently that Mrs Behn's plays have been rediscovered. In her own time her plays, which helped to introduce farce into the British theatre, were immensely popular.

[*Enter* FLORINDA *from the farther end of the scene, looking behind her.*]

FLORINDA   I am followed still. Ha! My brother too advancing this way! Good heavens defend me from being seen by him! [*She goes off.*]

[*Enter* WILLMORE, *and after him* VALERIA, *at a little distance.*]

WILLMORE   Ah, there she sails! She looks back as she were willing to be boarded; I'll warrant her prize. [*He goes out,* VALERIA *following.*]   5

[*Enter* HELLENA, *just as he goes out, with a page.*]

HELLENA   Ha, is not that my captain that has a woman in chase? 'Tis not Angellica. – Boy, follow those people at a distance, and bring me an account where they go in. [*Exit* PAGE.] I'll find his haunts, and plague him everywhere. Ha! My brother!

[BELVILE, WILLMORE, PEDRO *cross the stage;* HELLENA *runs off. Scene changes to another street. Enter* FLORINDA.]

FLORINDA   What shall I do? My brother now pursues me. Will no kind   10
power protect me from his tyranny? Ha! Here's a door open; I'll venture in, since nothing can be worse than to fall into his hands. My life and honor are at stake, and my necessity has no choice. [*She goes in.*]

[*Enter* VALERIA, *and* HELLENA's *page, peeping after* FLORINDA.]

PAGE   Here she went in; I shall remember this house. [*Exit boy.*]

VALERIA   This is Belvile's lodging; she's gone in as readily as if she   15
knew it. Ha! Here's that mad fellow again; I dare not venture in. I'll watch my opportunity. [*Goes aside.*]

[*Enter* WILLMORE, *gazing about him.*]

WILLMORE   I have lost her whereabouts. Pox on't, she must not 'scape me. [*Goes out.*]

You'll probably agree that this scene is anything but naturalistic. Characters are rushing on and off, speaking directly to the audience to let them know what they are thinking and doing.

● Try out the scene. As with *The Birthday Party*, the aim is to create the sense that things are happening very quickly, though instead of being all together in one room these characters are chasing each other over a whole town. How can the actors use movement and facial expressions to give the audience the idea that they are trying to catch or avoid each other as they run around a maze of streets?

● The scene has many of the hallmarks of a farce. Rearrange the lines in the box on page 163 and add your own stage directions to create a scene from another farce that would involve using the whole stage.

'Hello, darling.'   'My God! It's   'Darling!'   'Nigel!'
                     your husband!'

'Darling!'   'Quick! Hide!'   'Felicity!'   'Darling!'

'My God! The wife's   'What a surprise!'   'How lovely to
at home! Damn!'   see you!'

'Ah, er, hello!'   'Oh, God!'

Unit 44   The onstage audience

Dramatic irony involves the audience in the theatre knowing something that not
all of the characters on the stage know. In order to achieve this effect, it is sometimes necessary to position the characters on the stage very carefully.

In this scene from Shakespeare's *Julius Caesar*, a crowd of plebeians (common
folk) has gathered to hear why some of Caesar's most trusted friends have just
murdered him. Their leader, Brutus, has explained their reasons to the crowd,
who seem satisfied that they have done the right thing. But in this scene,
Caesar's friend, Mark Antony, who has been against the assassination, speaks to
the crowd. He has been warned not to say anything that will go against the assas-
sins, and has agreed, but notice how he works on the crowd here. At first they
seem wary of him and not all of them are willing to listen to what he has to say.
But as his speech goes on, they become more sympathetic to his argument and
end up on his side.

1ST PLEB   Say, ho! And let us hear Mark Antony.
3RD PLEB   Let him go up into the public chair.
    We'll hear him. Noble Antony, go up.
ANTONY   For Brutus' sake, I am beholding to you.
4TH PLEB   What does he say of Brutus?
3RD PLEB   He says, for Brutus' sake.   5
    He finds himself beholding to us all.
4TH PLEB   'Twere best he speak no harm of Brutus here!
1ST PLEB   This Caesar was a tyrant.

3RD PLEB   Nay, that's certain.
  We are blest that Rome is rid of him.
2ND PLEB   Peace! Let us hear what Antony can say.   10
ANTONY   You gentle Romans –
ALL   Peace, ho! Let us hear him.
ANTONY   Friends, Romans, countrymen, lend me your ears;
  I come to bury Caesar, not to praise him.
  The evil that men do lives after them,
  The good is oft interred with their bones;   15
  So let it be with Caesar. The noble Brutus
  Hath told you Caesar was ambitious.
  If it were so, it was a grievous fault.
  And grievously hath Caesar answered it.
  Here, under leave of Brutus and the rest –   20
  For Brutus is an honourable man;
  So are they all, all honourable men –
  Come I to speak in Caesar's funeral.
  He was my friend, faithful and just to me;
  But Brutus says he was ambitious,   25
  And Brutus is an honourable man.
  He hath brought many captives home to Rome,
  Whose ransom did the general coffers fill:
  Did this in Caesar seem ambitious?
  When that the poor have cried, Caesar hath wept;   30
  Ambition should be made of sterner stuff;
  Yet Brutus says he was ambitious,
  And Brutus is an honourable man.
  You all did see that on Lupercal
  I thrice presented him a kingly crown,   35
  Which he did thrice refuse. Was this ambition?
  Yet Brutus says he was ambitious,
  And sure he is an honourable man.
  I speak not to disprove what Brutus spoke,
  But here I am to speak what I do know.   40
  You all did love him once, not without cause;
  What cause withholds you then to mourn for him?
  O judgement, thou are fled to brutish beasts,
  And men have lost their reason! Bear with me,
  My heart is in the coffin there with Caesar,   45
  And I must pause till it come back to me.
1ST PLEB   Methinks there is much reason in his sayings.
2ND PLEB   If thou consider rightly of the matter,

Caesar has had great wrong.
3RD PLEB   Has he, masters!
I fear there will a worse come in his place.   50
4TH PLEB   Marked ye his words? He would not take the crown;
Therefore 'tis certain he was not ambitious.
1ST PLEB   If it be found so, some will dear abide it.
2ND PLEB   Poor soul! His eyes are red as fire with weeping.
3RD PLEB   There's not a nobler man in Rome than Antony.   55

● Pick out all the phrases spoken by both Mark Antony and the plebeians that tell you that not all of the crowd are listening to what he is saying at first.

● Do you think that the crowd should listen to his speech in absolute silence, or would there be moments when they might react? Perhaps at times they might nod in agreement or make some noises which show they are thinking about what is being said. Jot down some suggestions for how the crowd might react to certain lines.

● Where would you position the crowd on the stage? Mark out a space in your room to represent a stage. Decide where the theatre audience would be. What message would the audience get if Mark Antony was facing front and all the plebeians were facing him with their backs to the audience? How would it be if the crowd stood behind Mark Antony? Is there a way of making the theatre audience feel that they are part of the crowd that Mark Antony is talking to, yet still allowing them to watch the reactions of the onstage crowd? It's a tricky piece of staging: the theatre audience need to see how Mark Antony is operating but we're also interested in seeing the reaction of the crowd.

● Draw a diagram to show where you would position the actors so that the theatre audience would see and understand how the crowd change their opinion of Mark Antony.

● How do you feel about Mark Antony's argument? Do you think, fromwhat he says here, that it was wrong to kill Caesar? He says that Brutus is an honourable man; do you think he is? Do you think that Mark Antony really believes this himself or is he just saying it to keep himself out of trouble with Brutus and the others?

● Now, does your opinion of Mark Antony change when we tell you that at the end of the scene the plebeians rush off to rebel against Brutus and the others? Mark Antony turns to the theatre audience and says:

Now let it work. Mischief, thou art afoot,
Take thou what course thou wilt!

Perhaps, like the onstage crowd, the audience in the theatre have been taken in by his apparent sincerity!

Allowing the audience to see the reactions of an onstage audience can be crucially important and completely change our own reactions to the play. In Willy Russell's play *Our Day Out* the very last stage direction seems to change the whole play from one which is largely comic into something of a heartrending tragedy. The story involves a class going out on a day trip. The class are from a deprived inner-city area and the day out is a chance for them to get away from their miserable life in the city. Unfortunately, the Deputy Head – Mr Briggs – goes with them. He is a pretty miserable sort of bloke himself who doesn't know how to enjoy himself and seems determined to stop everyone else enjoying themselves too. However, after talking to one little girl – Carol – he realises why the kids hate him so much and tries to join in the fun for the rest of the day. He allows himself to be photographed by another teacher at a fun-fair and at the end of the play he offers to develop the film himself. Everyone, especially Carol, is pleased to see this new side of him.

This is the last stage direction:

Briggs has reached in his pocket for his car keys. The envelope containing the film comes out with the keys. He stands, looks at the envelope, opens it, takes out the canister and looks at it. He opens the canister and takes out the film. Suddenly deciding, he opens the film, exposing it to the light, before stuffing it into his pocket. He is suddenly aware of Carol, stood at the foot of the coach steps, watching him. He suddenly turns and strides past her, without a glance. She walks off clutching her goldfish in its plastic bag.

● Work in groups of three with one person playing Briggs, one Carol and the other as a director, trying to see the scene as a theatre audience would see it. Play out the scene in a number of different ways. How quickly should it be played? What should the actors do with their faces? Should Briggs start by smiling as he remembers the fun he has had and then realise what people might say when they see the photographs and turn to frowning? How does he look when he realises Carol has seen him destroy the film? Does Carol start by looking rather lovingly at Briggs? How and when should her face change?
● Improvise one of the following scenes and pay attention to where the characters should be positioned on the stage:
  Mr Briggs is explaining to another teacher that, sadly, the photographs haven't come out. Carol is listening.

Carol is telling the other children what she saw Briggs do. Briggs comes in and hears part of the conversation.

Briggs is trying to explain to Carol why he had to destroy the film. Their conversation is overheard by the teacher who trusted Briggs to develop the film.

Section five   Experiencing the production

Section summary

In this final set of units, the students are asked to consider how to assess their own experience of live theatre and given advice on how to write reviews and essays about plays. Particular attention is paid to comparing productions with their own knowledge of the printed text.

45   Attention seeking

Here the students are invited to consider the 'personal baggage' they take with themselves to a production and how this might affect their reading of the play on that occasion.

46   Just the ticket

In this unit, attention is drawn to the devices theatres use to try to shape an audience's attitude before the play actually starts.

47   Gut reactions

Stress is placed here on the audience's own personal and immediate response, which serves as a starting point to a more considered and objective assessment of the production.

48   Making a critical comment

A framework is offered here for students to note down key features of the production before moving on to structuring a written response to the play.

49   Reviewing the reviews

Finally, a unit is provided which draws the students' attention to the way in which published reviews may say as much about the reviewer's personal preferences as they do about the plays themselves.

Unit 45   Attention seeking

There are all sorts of reasons why you might go to the theatre. A very likely one is that you are studying the play and your teacher thinks it's a good idea for you to see it! Even if this is the case, your experience of the play in production will start long before the lights go down and the curtain goes up. You will be going along with certain expectations.

● Talk about all the things that you think might affect your enjoyment of the experience. For example:

Who am I going with?
Do I actually want to go?
How much is this costing?
How much do I know about the play already?

It's important to bear all of these things in mind – if you don't end up enjoying the show it might be because of them rather than the play itself! Your personal frame of mind is largely beyond the control of those putting on the performance.

● Look at the two posters on pages 170–171. Which one do you think might attract you to go and see the show?

● Knowing what you do about Shakespeare and the way many people react to his name, can you explain why the poster designers have used the images they have? What particular aspects of the play do you think they are trying to use to attract the audience?

● From looking at these posters, what sort of expectations would you have about:

how the play will be costumed
when and where the play will be set
what style of acting is likely to be used?

Any poster advertising a play will probably be a pretty good indication of the overall **production concept**, that is, the director's idea of how to do the show, what sort of atmosphere she wants to create for the audience and perhaps what particular theme or emotion she wants to explore. We're all very used to this because of the way films are advertised.

● Think of a play you know quite well and sketch a design for it. Your design should emphasise an aspect of the story that you find interesting and that would interest others.

The Merry Wives of Windsor

by **William Shakespeare**

Production sponsored
by Digital Equipment
Co Limited

Unit 46   Just the ticket

Let's face it, theatre tickets are usually pretty dull things which are simply used to tell you what seat you must sit on. Similarly, programmes tell you who is playing what part, what else the actors have been in and where you might eat a good curry after the show! (In truth, many programmes give you some very interesting background information about the play and the way it is being produced which can help a lot if you have to write about it afterwards.)

Sometimes, though, the tickets and programmes are used as part of the production concept. For example, in a play about the Second World War called *When the Lights Go On Again*, devised by a Year 10 group, the programmes were made to look like ration books. During the interval the audience had to present their ticket at a counter where they were told what they were allowed to eat and drink. They then had to queue at other counters where their ration books were ticked to make sure they didn't come back for any more!

In a production of Chris Bond's *The Blood of Dracula*, the programme was printed on a single large sheet of paper which included instructions on how to fold it into a crucifix – this came in handy when Dracula leapt from the stage and ran snarling around the auditorium!

● Bring in any theatre programmes you have kept. As a class, consider the different designs used and the sort of information they give.

● What sort of information or features do you find most interesting and useful in a programme? Think about a play you know well – one that has recently been performed in your school, perhaps – and make a 'mock-up' of your ideal programme for it.

● Look at the titles of the following plays. Can you think how tickets or programmes might be designed to help the audience get into the atmosphere of the play?

Sherlock Holmes and the Limehouse Horror (in which Holmes encounters the giant rat of Sumatra)

No More Sitting on the Old School Bench (life in the staff room of a comprehensive school)

Bouncers (a play about night club bouncers)

Zigger Zagger (a play about football supporters)

Stags and Hens (a play about, believe it or not, blokes on a stag night and girls on a hen night)

● Do you think that there are some plays where using the tickets and programmes in this way might be seen as no more than an unhelpful gimmick? What sort of plays would you think this sort of thing would be inappropriate for? Can you come up with any actual examples?

When you next go to see a play, try to sort out what the theatre is doing to affect the way you are approaching the production. Put these ideas alongside the other things that are affecting you personally about your visit.

Unit 47   Gut reactions

Look at these two responses to the same party:

———————————————

'It was brilliant! I got smashed out of my skull, got into a fight, was sick all down the hallway and woke up next morning in a bus shelter without my trousers on. Cool!'

'It was awful. People were getting horribly drunk and fighting. The house was swimming in vomit and I woke up next morning with a thumping head vowing never to do it again!'

———————————————

Does it sound like the kind of parties you go to?
● Make a list of things that you think would make a great party, then compare your list with those of three people in your group (don't choose your closest friends).
● Could there be any reasons why you personally wouldn't enjoy a party even though it had all the ingredients you've mentioned?
● Would your list hold true for every type of party? What if it was a wedding reception – perhaps your own wedding reception? What if it was a party to celebrate your younger sister's fifth birthday? Will this list still be true for you when you are celebrating your eightieth birthday? Talk about your criteria for a good party and why it might change.

There are a lot of factors here, aren't there? Some are to do with your own expectations, some to do with how other people behave and perhaps some to do with how you are personally feeling at the time. All of these things need to be considered when you are figuring out your responses to experiences, whether it's parties you've been to or plays you have seen or read.

So, what might your response to a particular play involve?

It could mean reacting to the play as it is in progress. Did you wet your seat with laughter or get nudged in the ribs because you were snoring so loudly?

It could mean clapping politely at the end or giving the actors a standing ovation and dozens of encores.

It could mean talking about the play afterwards to your friends.

It could mean – and we're only half-sorry for mentioning this – writing an essay or review of the play.

One thing is for sure, unless you are actually dead when you see a play you will be responding to it somehow. You will get a 'gut reaction' to it and there's nothing wrong in this. However, it can be interesting to reflect on your reactions further in order to figure out just why you had that reaction. Your reaction will doubtless be linked to your personal criteria about what makes a good play (though you may not have realised that you actually had any criteria). You will also already know from your own experience that your initial reactions can change over time because your personal criteria as to what is good or not have changed.

Shakespeare's play *Hamlet* is probably the most written about play ever. If you looked along the shelves of a university library you would find dozens of books devoted to this play alone. That's one heck of a response! Another extreme might be this:

'What did you think of it, then?'

'It was all right.'

A fair enough response, you might think, though would you feel the same way if you had performed in the play, or written it, or personally felt that it was the most moving experience of your entire life? Wouldn't you be intrigued to know why other people didn't feel the same way as you?

There's nothing more natural than wanting to talk about our experiences to check out how they match other people's responses. If you have something to say about a play, whether it's favourable or not, and you do it in writing or talk about it in a structured way your response is called a review.

Reviews can sometimes be gratuitously abusive. When the famous diarist Samuel Pepys went to see *Romeo and Juliet* in March 1662 he wrote:

'Romeo and Juliet' . . . is a play, of itself, the worst that I ever heard in my life.

In September of the same year he went to see *A Midsummer Night's Dream* and wrote:

174

. . . it is the most insipid, ridiculous play that I ever saw in my life.

Perhaps he was having a bad year! At least he had the excuse that he didn't know his diary would ever be published for others to read. Some critics still enjoy reviewing plays in the same way, though. Here is part of a review of a play called *Dracula*, starring Terence Stamp, which appeared in *The Times*:

Terence Stamp's 'Dracula' has nothing to offer apart from a noble profile. His entrances are insignificant, his voice without menace or mystery and his physical tricks consist largely of flapping his cloak, like a bat failing to take off.

These three reviews can be found, together with many more like them, in Diana Rigg's book *No Turn Unstoned*.
● If you were reviewing a school play in the school magazine, would you be so blunt in your comments? If not, why not?
● If you were being paid to write a review, would that make any difference to the way you spoke about it? Why?

Considering the circumstances in which you are writing a review is very important, as this will affect what you are saying and how you are saying it. What teachers and examiners are looking for in your reviews is that you've inspected your gut reactions to the play and can talk about what caused them.

Unit 48   Making a critical comment

A good way of sorting out your reactions is to start from the basics. You will be able to make some simple notes on some of these things before the actual performance of the play even starts. For example:
Title   What is the play called? What expectations does this set up for you?
Author   Who wrote it? Do you know anything about this writer? If so, does this give you any expectations?
Venue   Where is the play being performed? Does this suggest anything about how the play might be done and what sort of audience will be present?

175

Director and company   Are they famous? What other things have they done that might ring some bells for you? (Look in the programme to see what it says about them.)

Date   When is the performance? Is this in any way significant?

To consider the headings below, you'll have to pay attention in the theatre itself. You might sometimes see 'A' Level students desperately trying to scribble notes down in the dark. The trouble with this is that they might be missing bits of the play and failing to really get into it. It's probably better just to sit back and try to enjoy the experience, then make notes afterwards. Try jotting down straightforward notes on:

Staging   Was the play presented on a conventional stage? In the round? Among the audience?

Set   What was the set like? What did it show?

Costume and make-up   Were the characters set in some particular period? What colours were used? Were they realistic or in some way strange?

Lighting   Were lights used simply to illuminate the action or were there any special effects?

Sound   Was there any music? Were the sound effects simply functional (e.g. doorbells, telephone rings etc.) or were some of them strange in some way?

Acting performances   Were the actors believable in their roles? Could you hear what they were all saying and see what they were doing clearly? How well did they seem to communicate with you as an individual? Who was the star?

All of this information by itself will not make a particularly full or interesting review unless you add your own personal comments about how these different elements actually affected your enjoyment and understanding of the play. So, after making notes under the headings above, try using the following structure to produce a readable and well-informed personal response to the production:

Headline   Can you think of a snappy title which sums up your personal response?

Introduction   Try to grab the reader's interest by giving some details of what was really striking about the play. You may want to say something about what you thought were the main themes or concerns of the play and whether or not you thought these were in fact worth exploring.

Key facts   Focus on the specific aspects of the production that stand out in your notes as being worthy of comment. What caught your attention or surprised you? What seemed to you to be well done or confusing? Were there any individual actors who seemed more powerful than the rest and how did they achieve this?

In addition . . .   Add comments on any other points you think worth mentioning, for example, the context in which you saw the play might be relevant. Perhaps you had read the play beforehand and had a number of expectations that were shattered by this particular production.

Conclusion   Return to one or two of the ideas in your introduction and try to tie these in with your overall sense of the production so that the reader is clear about whether or not you liked the play and why.

● Now try to use this format to review a short piece of drama you have seen or perhaps been involved in recently. Give yourself a strict word limit – can you do it in 250 words?

It may be that you are asked to do more than just review one particular performance and write about the play as a whole. To do this you are obviously going to have to show a bit of knowledge! Making notes on the following will help you build a foundation for this:

Plot   Jot down in as few words as possible the story the play actually tells. Add your own comment about how interesting or relevant this seems to be to you.

Theme   Try to summarise what the play is really about to you. Does it seem to give a particular message or explore any particular aspects of human existence?

Genre   How would you describe this play when you put it alongside others you know? Is it a comedy, a tragedy, a historical play, a melodrama?

Structure   Does the play follow through a story in sequence or does it seem to jump around? Does it reach a climax at the end or are there a number of moments when the tension is very high? How does the play try to grab your attention? How does it try to affect the way you think about things?

Characterisation   Which characters do you find most interesting? Are they believable or do they have some other function that has perhaps given you a new insight into something?

Context   What do you know about when the play was written, who actually wrote it and under what circumstances?

You will see that comments can be made on these things just by reading the play. Your job, when you've actually seen the play in performance, is to judge whether or not the production has given you what you expected. If it hasn't, this might well be a good thing because it has made you see the play in a new way. On the other hand, you may feel that the production has simply made a bad job of the play – perhaps it has made the play more confusing or has simply been very badly performed. (Just why was Hamlet wearing pink fishnet tights and speaking in a Chinese accent? And why did he keep bumping into the scenery?)

Unit 49   Reviewing the reviews

What was the most recent film you went to see at the cinema? Why did you go?

It might be that you happened to be standing outside when there was a sudden downpour and you rushed in to stay dry – but we doubt it. The more likely answer is that someone told you the film was worth seeing. Perhaps it was a friend, or you had heard people talking about the film on television.

Did you think it was as good as they said? Better? Worse?

Reviews can help us make up our minds about whether or not going to see something will be worth our while, but you can't always trust everything you read.

- Read the reviews that follow, which are all of the same production. Talk about which one you think:

  gives you the most information about the play itself

  tells you most about the way the play is performed

  tells you most about the personal attitudes of the reviewer.

Perhaps you'll find that the ideal review is the one that has a balance of all three of these perspectives?

Michael Billington on a Death Of A Salesman that puts America on trial

Dream on, sucker

Lies or truth? Dreams or reality? Which do we live by? It is the great question that resounds through modern American drama: O'Neill, Miller, Williams, Albee, Shepard all supply different answers. But although it would be fascinating to see the National Theatre tackling one of its other manifestations, David

The classic

Thacker's Lyttleton revival of Death of a Salesman captures the poetic quality of Miller's attack on a corrupt, venal system.

I can't improve on Harold Clurman's original analysis of the play in 1949. He argued that the historical American

dream had been based on ideals of hard work and courage. Post-1900 that was distorted into the dream of business success: in particular, the fraudulence of salesmanship. The tragedy of Miller's hero, Will Loman, is that in becoming a salesman he suppresses his real persona. Ultimately he is destroyed by the ideology of the deal.

Miller's point is political as well as personal: indeed is still highly topical at a time when the ideal of salesmanship is so embedded in American life that it determines Presidential elections. The fundamental truth at the heart of Miller's play makes one overlook its obvious faults: that we never, in contrast to Mamet's Glengarry Glen Ross, see Willy Loman at work and that the downfall of his son, Biff, hinges too obviously on the discovery of his father's infidelity.

But the virtue of Miller's play is that it uses a fluid, dream-like form to convey Willy's evasion of reality. And that is what comes across strongly in Thacker's production and Fran Thompson's highly imaginative design. The elements of Willy's past are all eternally present, from the battered red Chevvy to the suspended bed containing his Boston mistress. The slowly revolving stage gradually brings each object into focus: even the central tree with its fractured trunk seems to symbolise the crucial split in Willy's personality.

Allowing for variable American accents, the acting is also good. Alun Armstrong as Willy, with his baggy suit and receding hair, has the look of a man who has driven too many miles for too many years in pursuit of a deal. The one element missing from his performance, discovered by Dustin Hoffman and Warren Mitchell, is the false, line-shooting perkiness of the younger man.

But Mark Strong is a fine Biff, steeped in the aura of failure, and there is authentic American support from Colin Stinton as Willy's cruelly myopic boss, for whom a tape-recorder is as much an executive toy as the latest computer would be today, and from Shane Rimmer as Willy's sympathetic neighbour. It's a well-staged revival that understands how Miller's social realism melts into the framework of a dream.

ON STAGE
– with George Cranford

A depressing tale – but stirring entertainment

DEATH OF A SALESMAN,
Lyttleton Theatre, London

EVEN if Arthur Miller's 1949 play is a depressing tale, it's not without humour and other ingredients for stirring entertainment.

National Theatre's production, directed by David Thacker, has Alun Armstrong in the central role of travelling salesman Willy Loman.

And how poignantly he shows Loman's loss of self-confidence, his sense of failure and awareness of growing old.

These feelings are contrasted in a series of flashbacks with happier, light-hearted and more hopeful moments of earlier years.

But low opinions of himself are not shared by his wife Linda – endearingly played by Marjorie Yatesby – who thinks he is 'the dearest man in the world'.

After crashing his car a couple of times, Loman is suspected of having a death wish.

Linda for a moment takes on a classical pose, declaring: 'Attention must finally be paid to such a man – he is not to be allowed to fall into his grave like a dog.'

And what of those dreams for his family?

His elder son Biff (Mark Strong) believes they were 'all the wrong dreams'.

His other son, Happy (Corey Johnson), wastes his father's efforts to give him a good start in life.

Believing in the American Dream, Loman replaces his feeling of failure with belief in his sons' future, but when these hopes are dashed, he makes his final exit to a brightly-lit space.

The door closes and the stage is dark.

And at his funeral, he is described as 'somebody way up there in the blue, riding on a smile and a shoeshine'.

REVIEWS

Rebirth of a legend

Over the years I've said some hard things about Arthur Miller, the self-proclaimed 'impatient moralist' who is still revered in this country but is accorded far less respect in his native America.

There are signs, however, that his saintly reputation is becoming dented even here, and I turned out for David Thacker's revival of Death of a Salesman (1949) expecting to be both bored and irritated by Miller's preachiness and clumsy stagecraft. But I have to report that this outstanding production, which I saw at the final preview, moved me, and many of my neighbours, to tears.

Thacker has become a Miller specialist and his great achievement here is to escape any sense of plodding naturalism. Fran Thompson's fine design is dominated by a big plane tree with a section cut out of its trunk. This might seem a clunking symbol of Willy Loman's rootlessness, but it creates the right disconcertingly dream-like atmosphere.

I'd never fully appreciated the fluid skill with which Miller interweaves

Theatre

DEATH OF A SALESMAN
National Theatre

past and present, as Loman finds himself torn between vivid memories and an intolerable present. Thacker's evocative production at Lyttleton Theatre, with its simple but stunning effective use of a revolve and haunting music by Adrian Johnston, creates a superb impression of Loman's confused, drifting mind.

Alun Armstrong gives a superb performance as Loman. It's not so much the despair as the terrible way he clings to the possibility of hope that is so moving. The final bruising scenes, in which he finally realises that his son Biff loves him, are almost unbearable to watch. Loman's sudden happiness is even more harrowing than his humiliating suffering.

Marjorie Yates is every bit as fine as his wife, who can easily seem like an idealised doormat. I have rarely seen unconditional love more touchingly conveyed on stage. Her tenderness, her fury with her

sons for their disgraceful treatment of their father and the final heart-catching scene are all wonderfully caught.

There's admirable support from Mark Strong as Biff, the son who finally comes to painful terms with both his father and his own failure. Corey Johnson is memorably persuasive as the despicable Happy. Even the supporting characters are played with fine attention to detail.

I still think there are moments when Miller announces his themes too portentously ('Attention, attention must be finally paid to such a person') and the unravelling of Loman's infidelity is clumsy. But in this production the play seems less like a finger-wagging parable about the cruelty of capitalism, and more like a devastating study of a family in torment. There is no mistaking the tremendous compassion at its heart and I left the theatre feeling ashamed of my past denigration of Arthur Miller. He can be an irritating playwright. On this occasion he is also a great one.

CHARLES SPENCER

181

Glossary

anagnorisis 'recognition leading to dénouement' (*Chambers English Dictionary*), i.e. the crucial stage on the character's journey through life; for example, when it dawns on Oedipus that he has done exactly what the prophecy said he would (see p. 145)

aside words spoken by a character to the audience that the others on stage are not supposed to hear (see p. 46)

auditorium the part of the theatre that accommodates the audience; it literally means 'the place for hearing' (see p. 15)

blocking going through the play planning the positions and moves of the actors; blocking is usually done at a fairly early stage of the rehearsals (see p. 14)

cameo originally a piece of jewellery depicting a head or a figure raised on a different coloured background; from this it came to mean a small but vivid part in a play or film (see p. 142)

caricature a **satire** on a person's appearance (e.g. a cartoon) (see p. 134)

chorus in Greek drama, a group of actors who comment on the main action of the play; in Elizabethan plays, the speaker of the prologue or other link passages, e.g. in *Romeo and Juliet* and *The Winter's Tale* (see p. 120)

cliché an idea, expression or plot which is predictably unoriginal, often because it is over-used (see p. 139)

conceit a fanciful idea; the word is related to concept; for example, when the audience is asked to believe something that is barely believable, such as an extraordinary coincidence (see p. 24)

context the surrounding situation or circumstances (see p. 34)

designer the person who is able to put the production concept into practice, taking the director's ideas and researching and creating designs for the set and costumes accordingly (see p. 15)

deuteragonist the second actor in a Greek tragedy (see **protagonist**)

dialogue words spoken by characters to each other, i.e. not a **monologue** or a **soliloquy** (see p. 37)

direct address when a character talks to the audience (see p. 44)

director the person with the overall **production concept**, who leads rehearsals and oversees the work of the set designer, costume designer etc. (see p. 15)

dramatic irony a situation in which the audience knows something that a character on stage does not; not to be confused with irony that is dramatic, i.e. something unexpected happening. Dramatic irony can be childishly funny, as in Punch and Judy; it can also be tragic, as in *Othello*, where the audience knows all the time that Othello's wife is not unfaithful to him (see p. 23)

dramatis personae a Latin phrase meaning, literally, 'the characters of the play', i.e. the list of characters (see p. 14)

farce a genre of comedy containing high-speed entrances and exits, misunderstandings and coincidences; see, for example, plays by Georges Feydeau, Ben Travers, Dario Fo; 'an extreme form of comedy in which laughter is raised at the expense of probability, particularly by horseplay and bodily assault' (*Concise Oxford Companion to the Theatre*) (see p. 67)

first person *I* or *we*, as opposed to *you* (second person), and *he/she/it/they* (third person); hence a first person narrative is a story told as if by one of the characters, as in *The Catcher in the Rye* and *The Great Gatsby* (see p. 6)

genre type or kind, usually of artistic or cultural products, such as films, television programmes, literary works, paintings and music (see p. 63)

medium (plural media) means of communication, usually to a mass audience, such as film, television, radio, the press, the internet (see p. 78)

melodrama (1) a type of play popular all over Europe in the 19th century, with larger than life elements, stereotyped characters and settings like ruined castles and haunted houses in the mountains; plays such as Planche's *The Brigand*, Boucicault's *The Shaughraun* and the anonymous *Maria Marten* fall into this genre (see p. 60)
(2) a style of theatre with exaggerated gestures and characterisation (see p. 114)

monologue a dramatic work or part of a play which consists of one character speaking (see p. 46)

motivation the character's deeper reasons for behaving as s/he does; often the motivation is obvious, but equally often it is a matter of interpretation. Some directors insist on the actors thinking deeply about their characters' motivation in rehearsal; to others it is only what they do and say on stage that matters. A famous actor, when asked by the director what his motivation was for crossing the stage, is supposed to have said that it was the prospect of getting paid at the end of the month (see p. 129)

narration telling the story, rather than enacting it (see p. 18)

naturalistic this is what most people mean when they say 'realistic'; looking and/or sounding real (see p. 70)

open stage   a stage with no **proscenium**, like the Olivier Theatre (see p. 104)

personification   giving personal qualities to something that is not a human being; in the case of plays, making something non-human into a character in a play, such as Sin in a morality play, or The Book in *The Hitchhiker's Guide to the Galaxy* (see p. 139)

play within a play   just what it says, really! You rarely find a complete play within a play, but to find parts of a play in some way dramatised within the main play is surprisingly common. *Hamlet* contains a famous example. There is usually some ironic parallel between the 'inner' and the 'outer' play (see p. 74)

plot   sequence of events that make up the story. The novelist E.M. Forster in his book *Aspects of the Novel* famously distinguished between story and plot like this: '*The king died and then the queen died* is a story. *The king died, and then the queen died of grief* is a plot.' But not everyone would make that distinction (see p. 12)

positioned   encouraged, as an audience, to look at the action in the play from a particular point of view; positioning usually affects your opinions and sympathies (see p. 70)

production concept   the overall idea or interpretation, linking design for set and costume, lighting, music and reading of character. Setting *The Merchant of Venice* in 1930s Germany, for instance, gives added point to the anti-Jewish feelings that some characters express during the play, and makes it likely that Shylock will be portrayed as a victim rather than a villain (see p. 169)

prologue   introductory speech giving the audience some idea of the story and perhaps the central themes of the play (see p. 10)

proscenium arch   the space (arch-shaped or rectangular) in the proscenium (the wall that divides the stage from the audience) through which the audience can see what is happening on stage; from this the phrase means the type of stage designed like this; see **fourth wall** (see p. 104)

protagonist   the first, and to begin with the only, actor in a Greek tragedy; because there were so few actors each had to play several parts, changing mask and costume for each character. The word is usually taken to mean the main character in a play (see p. 20)

proxemics   the art of using space, distance and closeness in a way which is meaningful; 'the study of the organisation of space' (*Batsford Dictionary of Drama*) (see p. 146)

satire   a work of theatre (or literature, or a media text) that ridicules a target (which might be a person, or a concept or another text) usually by means of exaggerated mimicry; known colloquially as a take-off, a send-up, a mickey-take, a spoof; different kinds of satire include **caricature**, parody, which is satire on style, and burlesque, which is a satire on a situation or event (see p. 63)

set 'the environment within which the actor performs; the term refers especially to the three-dimensional element of this' (*Batsford Dictionary of Drama*) (see p. 15)

SFX abbreviation meaning special effects

soliloquy a speech in which a character is talking to himself or herself during a play; the equivalent of an aria in an opera; not quite the same as a **monologue**, which is more complete in itself. *Hamlet* is famous for the Prince's soliloquies, especially the 'To be, or not to be . . .' speech (see p. 46)

soundscape using voices to do various simultaneous sound effects, giving atmosphere to a scene, such as a storm or beach party (see p. 35)

stage direction the part of a playscript that is not to be spoken aloud; the instructions for exits and entrances, or a set, and for how a character speaks, which are normally printed in italics or in brackets (or both) (see p. 7)

stereotype an immediately recognisable kind of character, such as the sneering, snobbish villain in Victorian melodrama (and in James Bond films), and the strong but sensitive man in television soap operas. Although stereotypes are, in a way, **clichés**, they are also found to be reassuring and therefore entertaining by many audiences (see p. 136)

stichomythia originally, in Greek plays, the type of dialogue where characters speak single complete lines of verse one after the other; in modern plays the term can be used to describe two characters speaking short phrases alternately. It is usually a sign of great dramatic tension, as in *Macbeth* Act 2 Scene 2 (when Macbeth has just committed murder) in which line 16 is split into four short speeches (see p. 55)

storyboard not to be confused with a comic strip, a storyboard is the shot-by-shot plan for a film, in which the picture to be seen is sketched in the frame, and beneath it is written information about camera angle and movement (if any), sound and lighting (see p. 83)

style distinctive manner of writing, acting, directing, designing etc. (see p. 67)

sub-text something that isn't actually stated, but that the audience understands; implications about a character's real thoughts, for example, or a developing relationship, which no one actually says (see p. 125)

symbolic   representing something other than itself; the witches in *Macbeth* could be taken to be symbolic of evil; the literal blindness of Oedipus is symbolic of his lack of understanding; the chopping down of the cherry orchard in the play called *The Cherry Orchard* is symbolic of the end of a whole way of life (see p. 107)

tritagonist   the third actor in a Greek tragedy (see **protagonist**)

Acknowledgements

With thanks to the following for permission to reproduce copyright material and photographs in this book:

Amber Lane Press for material from Martin Sherman, Bent (1979) pp. 36–7. Copyright (1979 Martin Sherman);

The Agency (London) Ltd on behalf of the authors for material from Alan Bleasdale, No More Sitting on the Old School Bench, Woodhouse Books (1979) pp. 21–2. Copyright (1979 Alan Bleasdale; and material from a version by Pam Gems of A Cherry Orchard by Chekhov, Cambridge University Press (1996) pp. 47–8. Copyright (1996 Pam Gems);

Alan Brodie Representation Ltd on behalf of the authors for material from John Godber and Jane Thornton, Shakers (1985) and BBC script of the same name (1992). Copyright (1984 John Godber and Jane Thornton);

Faber & Faber Ltd for material from Harold Pinter, The Room (1957); Harold Pinter, The Dumb Waiter (1957); Harold Pinter, The Birthday Party (1957); Peter Nichols, A Day in the Death of Joe Egg (1967); and Samuel Beckett, Waiting for Godot (1955);

Guardian Newspapers Ltd for Michael Billington, 'Dream on, Sucker', The Guardian, 2.10.96. Copyright (The Guardian 1996);

A M Heath & Co Ltd on behalf of the author for material from David Storey, Home (1970) pp. 2–3. Copyright (1970 David Storey);

Methuen Publishing Ltd for material from Howard Brenton, Epsom Downs, (Brenton Plays 1) (1977); Noel Coward, Blithe Spirit, (Coward Plays 4) (1979). Copyright (the Estate of Noel Coward; and Bertolt Brecht, Fear and Misery of the Third Reich, (Brecht Plays 4);

Nelson Thornes for material from C Bond, The Blood of Dracula (1995) pp. 39–40; Britton, Britton and Saunders, Work Ethic (1995) pp. 24–5; Lim Coghlan, A Feeling in my Bones (1992) pp. 2–3; and Brian Woolland, Gulliver (1993) pp. 3–4;

Peters Fraser & Dunlop Group Ltd on behalf of the author for Roger McGough, 'FX' from Rocking Duck by Roger McGough. Copyright (Roger McGough);

ACKNOWLEDGEMENTS

Radio Times for material from Radio Times, 12–18 October 1996;

Casarotto Ramsay & Associates Ltd on behalf of the author for material from Jack Rosenthal, P'Tang Yang Kipperbang (1984) pp. 54–5. Copyright (1984 Jack Rosenthal; and on behalf of The University of the South, Sewanee, Tennessee, for Tennessee Williams, The Glass Menagerie, New Directions (1959) pp. 234–235. Copyright (1945, renewed 1973 by The University of the South);

Reading Evening Post for review, 'On stage – with George Cranford', Reading Standard, 7.11.96;

Dee Conway 97, 160; Hulton Getty 103, 97, 161; Kobal Collection 159; Mary Evans Picture Library 97; National Theatre Archives 173; Royal Shakespeare Company 72; The Cartoon Centre, Kent / Bill McArthur 134 / Trog – Sunday Telegraph, 135

Every effort has been made to contact copyright holders. The publishers apologise to anyone whose rights have been inadvertently overlooked, and will be happy to rectify any errors or omissions.